The DYNAMICS of a WORSHIP LEADER

GABRIEL EZIASHI

The Dynamics of a Worship Leader.

Copyright © 2023 Gabriel Eziashi

ISBN: 9798394772672

Gabriel Eziashi
7027, Lake Jackson Drive,
Arlington, Texas, 76002,
United States of America.

Edited and Desktop Published by:
Rehoboth Consultancy Service
2304 Oak Lane, 3A Ste. #7
Grand Prairie, Texas, 75051
Tel: 972-742-7365
972-345-5357
www.rehobothbministries

Table of Contents

Foreword.. 1

Dedication... 5

Acknowledgments.. 7

Introduction... 10

01 | What is Worship? — 13

02 | The Importance of Worship — 24

03 | Worship in Other Capacities — 37

04 | Understanding Worship — 52

05 | Types of Worship — 57

06 | The Choir — 63

07 | Warning About Having a Choir — 71

08 | Characteristics of a Good Choir — 84

09 | Responsibilities of a Choir — 92

10 | Rehearsals Etiquette — 100

11 | The A-Z Tips on Voice Training — 106

12 | Making the Right Choices — 118

Bibliography — 124

Foreword

Bob Kauflin (November 2005) said the worship leader is "one who leads the congregation in the act of lifting their hearts and voices to God." This definition is definitely supported by the Scriptures with examples in **Psalm 95:1, 34:3**. In the NKJV, these say, ***"Oh come, let us sing to the LORD! Let us shout joyfully to the Rock of our salvation…Oh, magnify the LORD with me, And let us exalt His name together."*** The author of "The Dynamics of a Worship Leader" believes that humans were created for fellowship, from which intimacy is created, which, in turn, births worship. "Worship is a calling every human is endowed with from creation," Pastor Gabriel Eziashi said.

The focus of this book is not entirely on worship itself but on the dynamics of the worship leader. That is, how the worship leader actualizes moving others to lift their hearts and voices to God. To achieve this, the worship leader must not only understand for himself that worship is a mandate, privilege, weapon, and expensive, but also convincingly demonstrate that to others. One must love the LORD with all one's heart, soul, mind, and strength to offer one's entire being and existence as a living sacrifice that is holy and pleasing to God. Pastor Eziashi further said, "Faith is involved in worship because you can only give adoration to what you believe in, or else, that will simply be hypocrisy.

No hypocrite will have a place in [God's] Presence. So, as you worship in faith and holiness sacrificially, your worship shall be accepted by God as true worship!"

It makes sense that when the worship leader is able to move the heart and throne of God consistently over time, it will move the hearts of others in his sphere of influence to hunger for this experience themselves. Then, they are able to *"humble themselves and pray and seek God's face, turn from their wicked ways, that God will hear from heaven, and forgive their sin and heal their land"* (**2 Chronicles 7:14**, NIV, paraphrased). Such people can cry out to God and say, *"Search me, O God, and know my heart! Try me and know my thoughts! And see if there be any grievous way in me, and lead me in the way everlasting!"* (**Psalm 139:23-24**, ESV). Then, they are able to experience being *"filled with the knowledge of the glory of the LORD as the waters cover the sea"* (**Habakkuk 2:14**, NIV). When this happens, the individual is able to "know God, His timing, His voice, and His movements like Adam and Eve did" in the Garden of Eden before the fall, Pastor Eziashi said.

I pray for every reader of this book that the expectation of the one who desires that which is on the heart of the Father will be guided by **1 Corinthians 2:9** (BSB). It says, *"No eye has seen, no ear has heard, no heart has imagined, what God has prepared for those who love Him."* Amen. Read the book to be informed, use it to be wise, and recommend it to others so you can be a blessing.

Pastor (Dr.) James O. Fadel
Assistant General Overseer & Continental Overseer,
RCCG The Americas

Foreword II

This book, **The Dynamic of a Worship Leader**, is a must read. As a worship leader, I have discovered that many Bible theologians, scholars, and believers have written books on faith, holiness, breakthrough, prosperity, unrighteousness, prayers and other biblical titles, but only a few have written about the essence and importance of true worship of the Almighty God as analyzed by the author of this book.

Pastor Gabriel Eziashi has put together a resource material that does not only reveal his life as a veteran worship leader and music minister, but also encourages many that, as viable as prayer is, worship of the Almighty God is also a weapon of spiritual warfare.

This book reveals that worship is the heartbeat of God and should not be taken lightly. The author points out that worship is not cheap but an expensive venture that involves body, soul, and our spiritual being, and should be approached with all seriousness and hard work for those who desire to be involved in true worship of God.

The simple way the author presents this resource material for Worship leaders, Music ministers, Pastors, and Church leaders, will keep you captivated until you have finished reading.

The Dynamic of a Worship Leader will encourage you to evaluate your walk with God and make you realize that you need to spend more time praising and worshipping God, because in so doing your desires will be met.

I highly recommend this resource material to every Music director, Choir master, Worship leader, Music Minister, Choir member, and all who desire to jumpstart their life in the place of worship. Keep reading; do not stop until you have finished. Shalom!

Pastor John E. Omewah
Senior Pastor RCCG Heaven's Glorious Embassy Plano Texas USA; RCCG The Americas Continental Officer in charge of music.

Dedication

"Oh, taste and see that the Lord is good; Blessed is the man who trusts in Him"
(Ps 34:8 NKJV)

In the little time I have spent here on earth, the totality of my life epitomizes the scripture quoted above, as I have come across things I should not have seen, yet in the midst of the dire challenges I faced growing up, the Lord has been good to me. However, one thing I am also definitely sure about is that the Almighty God truly blesses those who trust Him, and I am ever overjoyed with the singular fact that He is faithful to me. To the glory of God, this is one of the reasons I gave my life to Jesus, at age twenty-one (21) and still going strong by His grace.

Hence, I dedicate this book to my Lord and Savior, the God who did not judge me when in my ignorance, stupidity, and feebleness, I walked in the path of destruction, rather He saw Christ Jesus' death on the cross and had compassion on me. To Him alone be all the glory and honor.

I also dedicate it to my immediate family starting with my wife Pastor (Mrs.) Oludayo S. Eziashi, who after the savior of my life, she is the second most precious person in my life. God gave me the choicest woman in the world to be my help meet. Even though, I had made loads of prayer requests in life, yet I could fondly remember only one of them which was that at age twenty-seven (27) I desired to be married to a woman that would keep me in Christ and remind me of God's faithfulness when I begin to drift in life.

I must confess, I had drifted a few times, but God had remained at work in me via this awesome angel, my wife. The irony is that she will never talk to me about my misdeeds but rather she will be on her knees in agonizing prayers for me and all I notice in me is change. I honestly can never thank her enough, as her love for me is reckless.

Can you believe in the same vein that I proposed to her in a prison during Prison Ministry assignment? Against all odds, her Church leaders, family members and other people who passionately cared for her tried to dissuade her from marrying me to no avail. Now after two decades of marriage and still counting God is still at work in us, and the union is blossoming daily. I love you dear and thank you for being a great standby.

To our children Miss Bryana and Mr. Yannis Eziashi, my number one fans and critics in all I do, I thank God for your lives, and the wonderful lady and gentleman He has made you guys to become. All I trusted God for was a family He can through me manage and handle, and to the glory of His holy name and you guys are the answers to my prayers.

Bryana, and Yannis, thank you for your constant support and encouragement, and my prayer for both of you is that God would make your children honor you too in Jesus mighty name. Thank You Lord for giving me this opportunity to be a husband, friend, and father to the greatest family on earth.

Acknowledgements

F irst and foremost, I acknowledge that everything I am today, is by and through the grace of God Almighty. I am not ashamed to say God has been at work in my life even from a tender age. You are reading this book today only by His work of grace and mercy in my life. If it had it not been for Him, I should have been dead at the age of sixteen (16) years, when I walked into an oncoming vehicle while trying to commit suicide. After the incident, I will never forget what the driver of the vehicle told me. He said, **"If you want to die, go home and die."** That statement till today jolted me back to reality and woke me up from my slumber.

I know very well that the story of my life would never have been complete without God working in me the way He did. God surrounded me with men and women who by His grace stepped into my life and began to shape and sharpen me into who I am today. Below is a list of a few of those men and women who in their capacity served as mentors, leaders, big brothers, and aunties. They divinely took turns by God's grace and supervision to mold my life and I want to thank and acknowledge them for building me up in God's word and work.

I begin with the General Overseer of the Redeemed Christian Church of God (RCCG Worldwide), Pastor, and Pastor (Mrs.) Enoch and Folu Adeboye, Pastor and Pastor (Mrs.) Ropo and Olayide Ropotusin,

Pastor Kingsley Alfred, Bishop, and Pastor (Mrs.) Yomi and Olive Olorunsaye, Pastor, and Pastor (Mrs.) Agu and Sola Irukwu, Canon and Judge Yemi and Simi Adedeji, Pastor, and Pastor (Mrs.) Sola and Grace Oludoyi, and my editor and his wife, Pastor and Dr. (Mrs.) Taiwo and Abidemi Ayeni.

I probably have never said thank you enough to these men and women as I should in the past. I have no idea where some of them are today, but I know and believe that someday, somehow, and somewhere someone will run into this book who knows them in person and help convey my sincere gratitude. Thank you, Sirs, and Ma'ams for your tireless work in my life. May God bless you all abundantly.

I also wish to acknowledge my siblings, the Eziashi's. Honestly, I would not ask for another family if I had the opportunity, because now I know better, that God could never have made a mistake in bringing us into the same fold. Despite all, we have been through, by His grace and mercy we are still standing under God's divine protection. Our parents Late Mr. and Mrs. James and Caroline Eziashi did their utmost best in providing us with all they could in life, and I only wished they lived long enough to eat the fruits of their labor.

I acknowledge my big brother and his wife, Pastor, and Pastor (Mrs.) Anthony and Bukola Eziashi, for stepping into the giant shoes of our parents. Miss Veronica James-Eziashi our eldest daughter, thank you for your tireless fight in seeing everyone grow and get better in life. Mr. Christopher James-Eziashi my immediate elder brother, you are simply the best, you always got my back. To Jude and Ambrose, my junior ones, I love you guys dearly, may God bless you all in Jesus' mighty name.

I also want to acknowledge some family friends and loved ones in the persons of Mr. and Pastor (Mrs.) Adebayo and Folake Adeleke, Mr. and Mrs. Henry and Folu Orji, Mr. and Mrs. Emeka and Saskia Agumadu, Miss Lolade Ogedengbe (My special daughter), Mr. and Mrs. David and Nike Toluhi. Miss Elizabeth Liga, and Mrs. Tosin Buraimoh. I could never have asked for better friends and loved ones than these ones.

Finally, I acknowledge the Household of Faith, Arlington family, and the body of Ministers with whom I faithfully serve. You are simply the best. Thank you all.

Worship is a calling every human is endowed with from creation. The main reason we were created was for fellowship, from fellowship intimacy was created, and intimacy births worship. The loose coinage for intimacy is "**Into me see**" which in other words means there is nothing hidden between both God and man as we worship Him in spirit and in truth "*...for the Father seeketh such to worship him.*" (John 4:23 KJV).

Worship may mean various things to several people, but regardless of what it means to you, please understand that worship is one of the greatest tools God has given to us for our use and purpose. There is literally nothing one cannot achieve using worship as a tool or a means to reach that goal. For example, you are seeking a job, and you have done everything you know to do, yet nothing seems to be coming forth. Right at this point I will encourage you to deploy the weapon of worship.

Let me share my personal story with you. My wife at a point was job hunting for a position in an organization and she had done everything she could possibly do, and I mean everything, but nothing was working. So, she informed me, and I could also see that she was getting to that point where everybody in the house was feeling the tension of what she was going through. So, I asked her to give me a day or two and thereafter I went into the place of worship. I know you might be wondering why go into the place of worship and not prayers. Straight up, understand that my wife is a woman of prayer and a worship leader too, I knew she had done all she could in prayers. The natural default to all Christians is prayer, but I found out that the reverse is God's original plan. You see God's mode of operation in the beginning was that Adam would do all he had to do in the garden, and in the evening, He would come and fellowship with him. The book of Genesis chapter 3, verse 8 says, *"When the cool evening breezes were blowing,* ***the man and his wife heard the LORD God walking about in the garden****. So, they hid from the LORD God among the trees."* (NLT)

Now do not focus on the later part of this scripture, rather I want us to review in part the portion that says, *"**When the cool evening breezes were blowing, the man and his wife heard the LORD God walking about in the garden…"***. This means that Adam and Eve knew God, His timing, His voice, and absolutely His movements. Not only did they know God, but there was also a close bond between them and Him. They were familiar with His movements in the garden, that they knew it was not that of any animal or of the devil who just led them to sin, rather it was God's.

Many of us at one point or another have relationship with God through His saving grace but beyond that God desires fellowship. This desire is so strong with God that it is emphasized without apologies by God in several portions of the Bible. For example, irrespective of how we feel about it, we are encouraged in Psalm 100 verse 2 to *"**Serve the Lord with gladness: Come before his presence with singing.**"* (NKJV)

It gladdens God's heart to see us worship Him in worship, praise, or thanksgiving. Those who know Him know that praising Him is His food and He takes or derives "*...pleasure in his people....*" (Ps. 149:4 NKJV). In fact, we are supposed to give Him pleasure, so why will anyone not want to give Him pleasure through his or her worship?

Brethren, even Adam and Eve knew this secret until sin knocked them out of fellowship with God. In the place of Worship, there is hardly anything you cannot receive from God if you know him. Always intentionally go into "*...his presence with thanksgiving And make a joyful noise unto him daily with Psalms.*" (Ps 95:2 NKJV).

Back to my testimony, day one passed, but by the close of work on day two my wife got a job, not the
one she applied for, rather they gave her something different with higher pay. All I did was worship the owner of all jobs and requested the one that would best suit His daughter so that she could be free to worship Him regularly and God did it!

Worship is a powerful tool or a weapon of war many believers have underutilized. This is because we only focus on worship to open our services and we leave it at that. Even in our private personal time with God we hardly spend quality time in worship with Him. However, those who know and understand how to use it well benefit immensely from the fruits of worship because God responds favorably to worship from the heart.

For the benefit of those who desire to go higher with God on this subject, we are thoroughly examining the question "What is Worship?" in Chapter One. You will all surely be blessed.

What is Worship?

CHAPTER 1

What is Worship?

Background Definition

The Hebrew word for worship is "*aboda*". It connotes worship as the following: fanaticism, cult, ritual, adoration, liturgy, work, job, employment, and labor. When literally translated it means "*service associated with the work done in the temple*". Temple in today's translation means heart, or life and that is the reason Apostle Paul in 1 Corinthians 3:16 says we "***...are the temple of God...***" (NKJV).

To understand worship is both to understand God and oneself. Worship is the entirety of man. The air we breathe, our minds, our bodies, our actions, our emotion, and our direct or indirect reactions to things or situations are all worship simply because it is a lifestyle.

Let's begin by looking at what the dictionary defines worship as! The Web dictionary defines Worship as:

"The reverence or adoration that one shows toward something or someone. It means to hold a person or object in high esteem or give a person or an object a place of importance or honor."

CHAPTER 1

But this cannot be the correct definition for a believer because there is a comparison between God, gods, and His subjects. God is superior to every other god, hence there is no basis for comparison. In Exodus 18:11, Jethro the father-in-law of Moses testified that:

"Now I know that the Lord is greater than all gods: for in the thing wherein they dealt proudly he was above them." (NKJV)

In fact, it goes against the standing commandment of God in Exodus 20:3 – 5.

"You shall have no other gods before Me. "You shall not make for yourself a carved image—any likeness of anything that is in heaven above, or that is in the earth beneath, or that is in the water under the earth; you shall not bow down to them nor serve them. For I, the Lord your God, am a jealous God, visiting the iniquity of the fathers upon the children to the third and fourth generations of those who hate Me" (NKJV).

The worship of God Almighty can never be aligned or compared with His creation. He created man in His image and likeness and this man who ought to appreciate Him for who He is through worship, instead foolishly carves his own idol and begins to offer it worship. The comparison of God with other gods is enraging to a true believer and to God Almighty, as seen in in Exodus 20:3 – 5. To further buttress this fact, we see the superior presence of God manifest in the book of 1 Samuel 5:3 – 5 when the Ark of the Covenant was captured by the Philistines, and they locked it up in the same room with Dagon their god! God's superiority obviously manifested because Dagon bowed to God's presence and got broken into pieces in the process.

"Then the Philistines took the ark of God and brought it from Ebenezer to Ashdod. When the Philistines took the ark of God, they brought it into the house of Dagon and set it by Dagon. And when the people of Ashdod arose early in the morning, there was Dagon, fallen on its face to the earth before the ark of the Lord. So they took Dagon and set it in its place again. And when they arose early the next morning, there was Dagon, fallen on its face to the ground before the ark of the Lord. The head of Dagon and both the palms of its hands were broken off on the threshold; only Dagon's torso was left of it. Therefore neither the priests of Dagon nor any who come into Dagon's house tread on the threshold of Dagon in Ashdod to this day" (1 Sam 5:1-5 NKJV).

So, what then is the acceptable definition of worship? Below are a few simplistic definitions yet loaded when properly understood:

- ✓ Worship is the nature of God. It is His person, that is how HE is. So, if we must WORSHIP! It must be according to how He wants it. (John 4:23-24)

- ✓ Worship is the cumulation of man's totality. It is the reason for man's creation, a means to foster fellowship and build intimacy between him and God.

- ✓ Worship is the lifestyle God created His believers to live, a way of life that epitomizes the person and the Kingdom of Heaven.

- ✓ Worship is a mandate, and all believers must worship God and Him alone.

✓ Worship is the act, designed not only to bring honor to God but also to bring a spirit of obedience and submission to the worshippers.

✓ Worship is the reason we were created, a lifetime of service, an opportunity, and a privilege to serve God Almighty and become a representative of His Kingdom.

✓ Worship is God's heartbeat, and He desires it, and He will do anything to have and keep true worship. True worshippers are expected to do so in spirit and truth (John 4:24).

✓ True worship is expensive. As the story goes, King Solomon sacrificed 144, 000 animals to God in one day, the question is "What is the equivalent of the cost of this sacrifice?"

✓ Worship is hard work. It is not as easy as it looks or sounds. To prepare for 15-minute worship for service, below are the steps to
follow:

  o Pray and Fast.
  o Selection of the songs.
  o Score and learn the songs.
  o Rehearse the songs!
  o Presentation of the songs in the right order.
  o Prayers for the manifestation of the Holy Spirit during ministration.
  o Recovery (*When you lead worship you become spent. You need the Holy Spirit to rejuvenate you*).

✓ God is worship because worship is Truth. Worship exposes or carries one into God's presence, and the more you are before God the more you become like Him.

✓ Worship is to show love and adoration to God Almighty.

✓ Worship is taking care of your body, as a lifestyle.

✓ Worship is speaking God's language.

✓ Worship is a weapon against Satan's tricks and lies.

Any one of the above definitions of worship can be accepted in Christendom and can serve as the beginning of many revelations to come as we explore worshipping God daily.

To have a deeper understanding of what worship is, I will expatiate the last three definitions stated above:

▪ Taking care of your body, as a lifestyle.

▪ Speaking God's language.

▪ A weapon against Satan's tricks and lies.

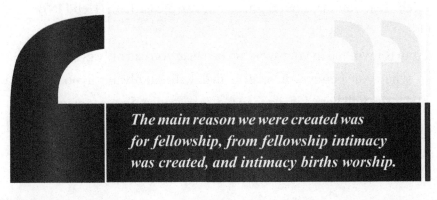

The main reason we were created was for fellowship, from fellowship intimacy was created, and intimacy births worship.

Taking Care of Your Body. as a Lifestyle.

I believe the average Christian seems to forget that our body is one of the most important tools God will use to further His work here on earth and that He cannot use a sickly or diseased body. It is time we begin to understand that our body is that vessel He will use to accomplish His plan and purpose for our lives. In Romans 12:1, Apostle Paul encourages us…

"Therefore, I urge you, brothers and sisters, in view of God's mercy, to offer your bodies as a living sacrifice, holy and pleasing to God — this is your true and proper worship." (NIV)

In breaking this down, true, and proper worship flow from pure vessels that house pure hearts. Your bodies must be prepared and presented as vessels of honor in selfless sacrifice to the living God. It must be a living sacrifice where with intentionality or deliberateness you surrender your all, in heartfelt worship without the vices of malice, unforgiveness, bitterness, envy, etc. standing in your way. It must be presented through a holy and pleasing vessel that God approves of. This is because without holiness no one can see Him (Heb 12:14) and without faith, no one can please Him (Heb 11:6).

Faith is involved in your worship because you can only give adoration to what you believe in or else that will simply be hypocrisy. No hypocrite will have his place in God's presence. So, as you worship in faith and holiness sacrificially, your worship shall be accepted by God as true worship! Anything outside of this is just noise, a useless one at that, not a joyful noise unto the Lord.

Along the same thought process of the importance of your body in worship, Rick Warren in his devotional book titled 'Transformation' said, and I quote:

"For change to happen in any area of your life, whether it's financial, vocational, educational, mental, or relational, you must begin with the physical (Body). Why? Because your body affects your behavior. Your muscles affect your moods and your motivation. Your physiology can affect your psychology".

In a nutshell, whatever controls your body, controls the essence or the outcome of your life. What you project, believe, say, or act on, are factors emanating from your body or vessel. Your behavior, moods, motivation and mental state (psychology) are all affected by the state of your body at any point in time. If you are in a bad mood for example and you do not control your emotion, your worship would be affected! It is the wholeness of the body that God desires in our worship, and He desires those that will worship Him in spirit and truth "***...for the Father seeketh such to worship him.***" (John 4:23 KJV)

For this reason, Rick asked a question and I never saw it this way before. He said, "W*hat does true and proper worship* mean to a worshipper?" He also gave insights from Romans 12:1. There are three things you can do with your body that the Bible says are acts of worship:

1.   Cleanse your body.
"Let us purify ourselves from everything that contaminates body and spirit, perfecting holiness out of reverence for God"
2 Corinthians 7:1 (NIV).

You cleanse your body by controlling what you allow in your mind through what you watch and listen to, and in your body by what you eat and drink.

So, "*Above all else, guard your heart, for everything you do flows from it.*" (Prov 4:23 NIV). The King James Version says, "*with all diligence...*". Meaning, do it with enthusiasm, without taking chances, making sure you dot your I's and cross your T's.

2. Care for your body.

> "*No one hates his own body but feeds and cares for it, just as Christ cares for the church*" Ephesians 5:29
> (NLT, second edition).

Keeping your body in shape is an act of worship to God.

Do physical exercise, take a prayer or praise/worship walk, maintain good eating habits by avoiding unnecessary snacks in between meals, and regular PH (personal hygiene). Have proper healthy habits and do not take unnecessary health risks by failing to do your yearly physical.

3. Control your body.

"*Each of you should learn to control your own body in a way that is holy and honorable.*" (1 Thess. 4:4 NIV).

Control your body so that it does not control you. There is no reason to say, "**I could not help myself!**" One of the things that put us under pressure and out of control is what we see, hear, or think about. As a man, if you subject your eyes and mind to ex-rated movies or the habit of looking at skimpily dressed ladies, one day you would lose control and find yourself sinning against your body before you know it. Just watching is already a sin, then giving it a thought is exacerbating before the Lord. Anybody who engages in this kind of bad habit falls deep unless they have divine intervention.

Learn to say NO! Whether it be for food, bodily urges, or non-edifying relationships. Keep your body in check and you will be able to offer unto God true worship.

Beloved, no matter what kind of change you want to make in life, it will take hard work, diligence and focus to achieve it. This means energy is required and to have the energy to meet your goals, change must start with your body.

Speaking God's Language.

When we choose to worship and praise God always, (especially during a trial) what we are simply saying is that we choose God above our trial or tribulation. We are saying we choose His presence instead of the prevailing circumstance. Such was the case of Paul and Silas when they were in prison.

Prison spells anger, depression, and rejection. It amplifies failure and the worst of anything that can happen to a 'man'. Instead of focusing on their situation, these guys turned it around and sang praises to God. They simply chose to speak the language of God where He was magnified, and their pain was relegated to the background. They took solace in giving God pleasure, because of their worship, God showed up and delivered them from bondage!

We read about their testimony in Acts 16:25-26 (NKJV):

"But at midnight Paul and Silas were praying and singing hymns to God, and the prisoners were listening to them. Suddenly there was a great earthquake so that the foundations of the prison were shaken, and immediately all the doors were opened, and everyone's chains were loosed."

Worship should always be our response to life because when God is lifted, He draws everything to Himself:

"And I, if I am lifted up from the earth, I will draw all peoples to Myself" (John 12:32 NKJV)

Remember, God's plan for us is for good and not evil, and whenever we adulate Him, He shows up because He inhabits the worship and praises of His people.

A weapon against Satan's tricks and lies.

The situation of Paul and Silas shows us that even when faced with trials and tribulations, we are to worship and praise God. Another good example is King Jehoshaphat in the book of 2 Chronicles Chapter 20. Three kings from the nations of Ammon, Moab, and Mount Seir came against Israel for war.

I mean how do you deal with not one, not two, but three enemies coming against you at the same time? The move alone is enough to cripple any nation. But this was not the case for King Jehoshaphat because he knew His God, he worshipped and praised him regularly. God showed up and that battle was won without lifting a finger.

The fact is the choice to put God first in a time of battle or a challenge. Like in the case of David and Goliath in the book of 1 Samuel chapter 17. David's decision to put God first switched the entire situation from a physical to a Spiritual battle. This means God now fights in your place.

The question now is when God fights for you who do you think will win? God of course! So let us learn to put God first in all our endeavors in life by worshipping Him recklessly.

Worship will always put a spin on all matters no matter how bad it gets. Always remember, Worship is a Weapon of War!

The Importance of Worship

CHAPTER

2

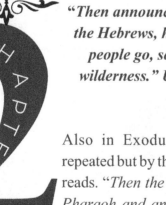

The Importance of Worship

A. Worship is Needful

Worship is so important to God that a whole nation was brought down to its knees because of it. If you read the book of Exodus from Chapters 2 verse 11 through to Chapter 12, the nation of Egypt experienced the depth of God's wrath just so His children, the Israelites, would be released to Worship Him.

God will go to any length to get a true and pure worshiper to worship Him. For example, in Exodus 7:16 (NLT), Moses announces God's desire to Pharaoh, he said,

"Then announce to him, 'The Lord, the God of the Hebrews, has sent me to tell you, "Let my people go, so they can worship me in the wilderness." Until now, you have refused to listen to him".

Also in Exodus 8:1, the announcement was repeated but by this time the tone was assertive, as it reads. *"Then the Lord said to Moses, "Go back to Pharaoh and announce to him, 'This is what the Lord says:* ***Let my people go, so they can worship me"*** (NLT).

CHAPTER 2

25

We all know the end of this story; the nation Egypt was brought down to her knees and God got His children out of that nation so they could worship Him. In total ten plagues were unleashed on Egypt:

1. Their water turned to blood, the water stank, and the fish died.
2. They were invaded by frogs that later died and their bodies stank.
3. The dust of the earth became lice throughout all of Egypt, so there were lice on all the Egyptians and their animals.
4. The affliction of the swarm of flies everywhere.
5. Severe pestilence struck their livestock dead.
6. Boils and skin sores broke out all over their bodies and their animals.
7. A violent hailstorm destroyed their crops.
8. A swarm of locusts ate what was left in the land.
9. Darkness that could be felt covered the nation of Egypt for three days.
10. The death of their firstborn children, servant's children, and all firstborn animals.

All these were released over the stubborn Egyptian overlords and their people just so that God could be worshipped by His people. If you are still thinking worship is nothing, you really need to reconsider your stand because that same God is still God today. Hebrews 13:8 (NLT) says, "*Jesus Christ is the same yesterday, today, and forever*". Just a note of warning, do not trifle with God when it comes to worship.

Worship is not just what God loves; He demands it. Even the Lord Jesus told the woman at the well that God is seeking those who will worship Him in spirit and truth (John 4:24). Also, in Hebrews 13:15, Paul encourages us to continually offer the sacrifices of praise with thanksgiving unto God. In fact, he tagged it "*the fruit of our lips*", while Hosea declares it as "*…so we will render the calves of our lips.*" (Hosea 14:2 NJKV). The "*calves of our lips*" is a metaphor for the "*sacrifice of praise.*" Worship embodies praise and thanksgiving, and God desires to see us engaged in them all.

The importance of worship can never be over-emphasized for various reasons. Worship is so powerful that it can shift one's mindset and change our perspective about things. The deeper you worship the higher the realms of the revelation of God are unveiled to you about you and the world you live in. Deuteronomy 29:29 says,

"*The secret things belong to the LORD our God, but those things which are revealed belong to us and to our children forever, that we may do all the words of this law*" (NIV).

You can only search out secret things when you are willing to pay the price and only those who fear Him by expressing it in true worship have His secrets revealed to them. God both loves to operate in deeper relationships and fellowship so, those who honor Him with their worship are given the opportunity to see things ordinary folks do not see and this is because:

"*The secret of the Lord is with them that fear him; And he will shew them his covenant.*" (Ps 25:14 NKJV)

When you worship, you trigger the opening of the windows of heaven over you and there is nothing you ask for that will not be answered because not everybody can access heaven just like that. Those who regularly do so because they fear and love the Lord are in essence saying:

> "*Mine eyes are ever toward the Lord; For he shall pluck my feet out of the net.*" (Ps 25:15 NKJV)

In a nutshell, "*Mine eyes are ever towards the Lord;*" in the literal sense means "My eyes are ever lifted in worship towards the Lord." Recall the counsel of Paul in 1 Timothy 2:8 (KJV)? "*I will that men pray everywhere, lifting up holy hands....*". This simply is a call to surrendered worship and those who do connect with God's open heavens and secrets.

It is therefore not surprising that Prophet Elisha, when confronted by a difficult request asked for a worshipper.

> "*But now bring me a minstrel. And it came to pass, when the minstrel played, that the hand of the Lord came upon him*". (2 Kings 3:15 KJV).

The story behind this incident was that the Kings of Israel, Judah, and Edom went to war against Moab, but they had no water for their fighting army. So, in their predicament, they panicked, and Jehoshaphat was inspired to ask:

> "*Is there not here a prophet of the Lord, that we may enquire of the Lord by him?...*" (2 Kings 3:11 KJV).

One of the King of Israel's servants told him Elisha was in that town and they all went down to town to look for him.

After Elisha's initial resentment in responding to them because of the King of Israel, he took the challenge up because of Jehoshaphat the King of Judah. Elisha understood the mind of God and what triggers the hands of God to move for those who fear Him. The moment the worshipper he sent for began to engage God in worship God spoke through Elisha and the answer to the problem that held the whole nation captive was about to follow.

"And he said, Thus saith the Lord, Make this valley full of ditches. For thus saith the Lord, Ye shall not see wind, neither shall ye see rain; yet that valley shall be filled with water, that ye may drink, both ye, and your cattle, and your beasts."
(vs. 16-17 KJV).

Worship can do anything; it can order one's step into their destiny. It can bring instant healing on sicknesses, infirmities, or generational curses, causing a permanent change in the family. Worship gives access to both God and man because it is in the place of worship, we can hear God loud and clear.

Worship opened the heaven for Elisha to make a prophetic proclamation as the anointing of God came upon him. He needed worship as a primer to connect with God in an open Heaven experience. He was not disappointed in his expectation and the people as well were assured of winning the war against Moab because "*...it came to pass in the morning, when the meat offering was offered, that, behold, there came water by the way of Edom, and the country was filled with water.*" (v20 KJV)

Whether you want to believe it or not, worship is an important weapon of war God has given us to operate as overcomers in the land. Worship matters to God, to you and me because He wants to see us succeed. If we can apply the weapon of worship the losses, we have suffered in life would probably have not occurred.

Even though some of us do worship, the only issue we face is that we allow personal distractions to get in the way. We allow the world to fill us up with issues we have no power over, and we take it into the place of worship, and as a result, the answer to our prayers is always futile. This is because God is a Spirit and those who must worship Him must do so in spirit and in truth (John 4:23).

Bringing malice, resentment, unforgiveness, hatred, and so on into the throne room of worship is tantamount to worshipping God in the flesh. This is **SIN** in capital letters and as the New International Version of John 9:31 (NIV) reveals to us:

"We know that God does not listen to sinners. He listens to the godly person who does his will."

It is important to know what true worship is and the atmosphere wherein we can engage God in worship. God wants the totality of ourselves and not just part of us. He can never tolerate sharing you with the vices of the flesh. So, know this for sure.

Most times we often take singing, clapping, or listening to sermons to mean worship, but those are just elements of worship. They are activities that worship was factored into. Worship is a lifestyle, a gathering of believers whose beliefs are based on one God. Praise is good but it is just an expression we give to 'worship'.

> *Bringing malice, resentment, unforgiveness, hatred, and so on into the throne room of worship is tantamount to worshipping God in the flesh.*

B. Reasons Why Worship is Important

1. To Worship involves Total Surrender of our Lives to God.

As mentioned earlier, God desires and demands surrendered worship. For this reason, worship demands commitment, obedience, and diligence from the worshipper. The reason is you cannot worship what or who you do not know. A phrase that best describes this point is being totally "Sold Out" to the Lord. No wonder Apostle Paul encourages in Romans 12:1 saying,

"I urge you, brothers and sisters, in view of God's mercy, to offer your bodies as a living sacrifice, holy and pleasing to God—this is your true and proper worship." (NIV).

This paints for us the picture of surrendered sacrificial worship with the wholeness of our being in His presence! A sacrificial lamb does not struggle, it is not distracted, and neither is it polluted but set apart for worship. To please God, you must meet this expectation which He has given you the grace to attain.

2. To Worship is to Put Our Attention on God

True worship is based on the desire to honor God from our hearts in true surrender to His will. It requires a personal revelation of God as found in the Scriptures. Worship is not based on my likes or dislikes. It is not based on my personal preferences or priorities. The revelation you have or know of the God you worship makes a difference. Jesus Christ in Luke 9:16-17 (NKJV) looked unto God to feed His people as we read below,

"Then He took the five loaves and the two fish, and looking up to heaven, He blessed and broke them, and gave them to the disciples to set before the multitude. So, they all ate and were filled, and twelve baskets of the leftover fragments were taken up by them".

Here is the example of Jesus with surrendered heart in sacrificial worship lifting holy hands without wrath and doubting expecting that the Father would answer His request and He did. The bread and fish multiplied so much that they had twelve to-go baskets after they had all eaten to their fullest. Worship is the key to a miracle.

3. To Worship Involves 'Dying to the Flesh'.

The flesh is always at war with our spirit man. So, as we are warned in the scriptures, we must do all we can to stop the flesh from ruling over our spirit. Therefore, *"Keep thy heart with all diligence; For out of it are the issues of life."* (Prov 4:23 KJV). We must learn to remove ourselves, our worries, our opinion, and our questions when we worship. Meaning that we must allow our asking and thinking to align according to the power that works in us (Eph 3:20).

In that way we will experience sincere and unpolluted sacrificial worship, thereby giving God the appropriate honor due to His name. The expectation to honor God in our worship is clear in the scriptures but let us see David's counsel in Psalm 29:1-2:

> *"Give unto the Lord, O ye mighty, give unto the Lord glory and strength. Give unto the Lord the glory due unto his name; Worship the Lord in the beauty of holiness."* (NKJV)

Our example, the Lord Jesus at every opportunity gives honor to God. In Luke 22:42-44 (NKJV); He was facing death, yet He put that aside and focused on giving honor to God.

> *"Father, if it is Your will, take this cup away from Me; nevertheless, not My will, but Yours, be done." Then an angel appeared to Him from heaven, strengthening Him. And being in agony, He prayed more earnestly. Then His sweat became like great drops of blood falling down to the ground."* (NKJV)

The only way to be happy in the Lord is to trust and obey. Jesus exemplified this and so we have no excuse.

4. To Worship Involves Personal Sacrifice

Praise is easy when times are good. When everything is working out as desired, but when things go south, praise barely speaks as we lack the motivation and faith to do so. Our natural disposition is to praise God for whatever He has done in our lives and when these fail, we turn cold toward Him. Worship on the other hand weathers all storms, as it requires us to worship Him for who He is to us, and it does not matter whether He had done something for us or not. We sacrificially worship Him because we fear and love Him.

For this reason, we put aside our feelings or pain to worship God in spirit and in truth. Job got this right when he said in Job 13:15 (NKJV):

"Though He slay me, yet will I trust Him. Even so, I will defend my own ways before Him".

At this point Job has lost everything; from children to businesses whatever you can think of, he lost. Yet his trust and belief in God was unwavering, that is trust founded on resolute faith at work and this is God's expectation for us too.

5. We Must Worship in the Face of Pain and Loss

One of the quickest ways to heal when life throws a curved ball at one is to worship. Because at that point there is a supernatural exchange between God and the one in pain. King David showed this maturity to worship when he lost a child that was conceived in adultery. He prayed, but the child still died so in 2 Samuel 12:20 (NKJV) the Bible says:

"So David arose from the ground, washed and anointed himself, and changed his clothes; and he went into the house of the LORD and worshiped. Then he went to his own house; and when he requested, they set food before him, and he ate".

It is highly imperative that we know and understand that pain and loss are a part of life. One can never use worship to try and manipulate God into doing his or her wish. God is not a man; He cannot lie or change to suit man. No matter what happens God remains God.

6. To Worship Is to Celebrate God for who He is and Praise Him for All that He does for us.

Words honestly fail me in trying to convey such a great God, but still, will I yet praise Him. The reason for perpetually praising Him is that it could have been worse. I really need you to take a break and look at those things you have complained about and ask yourselves this question. Are there people going through things worse than this? The answer is always yes. Therefore, King David wrote in the book of Psalm 124:1- 5:

"If it had not been the Lord who was on our side," Let Israel now say "If it had not been the Lord who was on our side, When men rose up against us, Then they would have swallowed us alive, When their wrath was kindled against us; Then the waters would have overwhelmed us, The stream would have gone over our soul; Then the swollen waters Would have gone over our soul" (NKJV).

But how did David get to this point of resolute and unshakeable faith? He had faced numerous challenges in life that made him look to God for help alone. In fact, he said in Psalm 27:13-14:

"I had fainted, Unless I had believed to see the goodness of the Lord in the land of the living. Wait on the Lord: Be of good courage, and he shall strengthen thine heart: wait, I say, on the Lord." (KJV)

He discovered and declared these secrets in Psalm 27:13-14 and by the time he got to Psalm 124:1-5 he was giving testimony of God's goodness.

The secrets in Psalm 27:13-14 are itemized below:

The secrets are:

i)   Have Faith and be convicted in what you believe.

ii) You must always see through the eyes of faith, the positive side of things. In Mark chapter 9 and verse 24 sights the fact that it is possible to partially believe in something or someone. So, it reads; *"Immediately the father of the child cried out and said with tears, "Lord, I believe; help my unbelief!"*.

iii) Wait on the Lord (Is 40:31)

iv) Be of good courage and do not fear.

v)   Wait for the Lord (Micah 7:7)

> *One can never use worship to try and manipulate God into doing his or her wish. God is not a man; He cannot lie or change to suit man.*

Worship in Other Capacities

CHAPTER 3

W orship is way much deeper than a human being could imagine. The Bible talks about mysteries of the Kingdom of God, and I absolutely believe that worship is one of those mysteries. The reason is that worship can easily switch from one realm to another as it is allowed to function in its fullness. To buttress this affirmation, let us look at worship from other perspectives or capacities.

A.Other Perspectives of Worship

1. Worship in the place of Prayers.

As far as I am concerned, worship is a form of prayer, only that it is been said in the form of singing. Or better still, worship is a prayer you sing! For example, in the face of adversity, worship has a way of switching things around. Apostle Paul and Silas were in prison, they prayed and after a while, they switched to worship and began to sing (Acts 16:25-26). Only then did something miraculous happen. They moved worded prayer to the level of kingdom worship praying in spirit and in truth without offense. This truly is the kind of worship that God Himself seeks! (Jn 4:23) The account of this high-level worship is found in the book of Acts 16:25-26 (KJV):

"And at midnight Paul and Silas prayed and sang praises unto God: and the prisoners heard them. And suddenly there was a great earthquake, so that the foundations of the prison were shaken: and immediately all the doors were opened, and everyone's bands were loosed."

Please, do not misunderstand me, I am in no way trivializing prayers or the potency of prayer. I am only saying when worship is introduced to prayers, there seems to be a shift in the spiritual realms that causes the atmosphere to give way for God's glory to come down. Even God recommended it as a potent weapon of war during the attack of the children of Moab, Ammon, and Mount Seir against small Judah. We will see this reviewed in the next subtitle, please join me.

2. Worship as a Weapon of Warfare

The beautiful thing about worship is that it has nothing to do with one's ability to sing on keys, or to be acquainted with the tones of music. So, when using worship as a weapon of warfare please understand that before you begin, heaven is already waiting to join you in the war, because the Holy Spirit inspired it in the first place.
There is no better scripture to further drive this point home than the one found in the book of 2 Chronicles 20:20 – 24:

"So they rose early in the morning and went out into the Wilderness of Tekoa; and as they went out, Jehoshaphat stood and said, "Hear me, O Judah and you inhabitants of Jerusalem: Believe in the Lord your God, and you shall be established; believe His prophets, and you shall prosper." And when he had consulted with the people, he appointed those who should sing to the Lord, and who should praise the beauty of holiness, as they went out before the army and were saying:

"Praise the Lord, For His mercy endures forever." Now when they began to sing and to praise, the Lord set ambushes against the people of Ammon, Moab, and Mount Seir, who had come against Judah; and they were defeated. For the people of Ammon and Moab stood up against the inhabitants of Mount Seir to utterly kill and destroy them. And when they had made an end of the inhabitants of Seir, they helped to destroy one another. So when Judah came to a place overlooking the wilderness, they looked toward the multitude; and there were their dead bodies, fallen on the earth. No one had escaped." (NKJV)

Worship when used as a warfare tool has a way of settling issues even without one's involvement, because it shows that one trusts God enough to handle the situation at hand. I am a living testament of God's goodness as I have used worship as a warfare tool and the results still lives on seventeen years later. I personally recommend it and encourage you to key into the art of worship.

3. Worship as a Weapon of Breaking Fallow Grounds.
For clarity purposes, I will give a little definition to these words – "**Fallow**" and "**Ground**".

a) Fallow means something that has been left unused for a while.
b) Ground on the other hand is a place, a land, oil, or state of a thing.

If we knit both definitions together, it will go thus,

"A Fallow Ground is a place, a land, or soil, which has been left unused or untended for a period. In other words, it has been left dormant for a time."

The question then is how does worship relate to breaking fallow grounds? To answer this question let us put things in perspective.

- ➤ While Fallow represents the state of the heart.
- ➤ The Ground represents the heart of a man.

Worship as we know by now is a lifestyle, the way to live life to the fullest, and live it continually in the presence of God. If for any reason, there is a break in that relationship or intimacy with God a separation happens, even without the knowledge of the man sometimes. The quickest way to resolve that break or space is through repentance and worship. Prayer is good but God cannot resist true worship from a pure heart crying Abba Father. Romans 8:15(NKJV) puts it this way:

"For you did not receive the spirit of bondage again to fear, but you received the Spirit of adoption by whom we cry out, "Abba, Father".

Never ever give space or room for there to be a break between you and God Almighty, because, at every given point, man is answerable to someone. Your relationship and fellowship with God are so important because God created you for worship! He demonstrated that in the Garden of Eden where He always went to have fellowship with Adam and Eve.

Becoming cold on God is a dangerous place to be and Revelation 3:15 and 16 (NKJV)confirm it.

"I know your works, that you are neither cold nor hot. I could wish you were cold or hot. So then, because you are lukewarm, and neither cold nor hot, I will vomit you out of My mouth."

God keeps His word, and He will do exactly as He promised to a lukewarm soul. Please understand that the devil is not happy that man worships God because he knows such worship strengthens man's relationship with God. So, one of the paramount jobs of the devil is to stop the man from worship at all costs. We see his strategic effort revealed to us in John chapter 10:10 (NKJV),

"The thief does not come except to steal, and to kill, and to destroy. I have come that they may have life, and that they may have it more abundantly."

The job description of the devil is clear, and he is adept at reaching his goals. The beginning of his evil actions sprang out of pride, and he lost all the rights and privileges he enjoyed in the presence of God as the anointed Cherub who worshipped in God's presence as other angels did. In fact, the Bible describes him in Ezekiel 28:13 as a walking instrument of music as God endowed him with such beauty and grace that inspired the root of his pride:

"The workmanship of thy tabrets and of thy pipes was prepared in thee in the day that thou wast created." (Ezek. 28:13 KJV)

God loves worship, and so, He created one who could be part of the worship in heaven, but his beauty got into his head and God had to cut him to size. He was perfect in his ways from the day he was created until iniquity was found in him. His heart was lifted against God, and he said in his heart *"…I will ascend into heaven, I will exalt my throne above the stars of God…"* (Full references of his activities are found in Isaiah 14:12-17; and Ezekiel 28:14-17 NKJV).

The reason for this background information is so that we never take God for granted. No one is indispensable in His sight. At the same time guard your heart with all diligence because the root of rebellion springs up from there. Never leave it fallow or unattended to, Satan will take advantage if you do. Remember, **"An idle mind is the devil's workshop."** That is the reason we are encouraged to meditate or engage our hearts in worship, praise, or thanksgiving at every opportunity because your heart is the throne room of God.

4. Worship in Prophetic Grace and Utterance.

Just like every other gift or office in the body of Christ, Worship is also a major force or gift and there are various reasons for this. Worship grants access to the throne room quicker than we can imagine. There are levels or realms one gets to, and you unlock gifts or giftings. The more dedicated you worship God, the higher He draws you closer to Him. The closer you get the more revelation and messages you receive because you can be trusted to handle what is been given to you to deliver or keep as information only. The entire book of Revelation was written based on revelation given to Apostle John in Patmos while he was in exile. Apostle Paul wrote Timothy in the book of 1 Timothy 4:14 (NKJV), saying,

"Do not neglect the gift that is in you, which was given to you by prophecy with the laying on of the hands of the eldership".

Every believer carries a measure of this gift of worship, and to attain the realm where we function at the level of the prophetic, grace, and utterance comes with time and commitment to God. This gift can be activated when you are resolute in your heart that it's God alone.

I must sound a note of warning here because as much as I desire that every worshipper walks in this prophetic grace and utterance, there is nothing as beautiful as when you are in a meeting and during worship your issues are addressed by God. It is also important to mention that you need to be careful here because this gift is one of the most abused gifts in the body of Christ. So, watch and pray, test every spirit. Ask yourself the question **"Is the speaker a true man or woman of God or a fake?"** In 1 John 4:1- 3 (NKJV), we are warned:

"Beloved, do not believe every spirit but test the spirits, whether they are of God, because many false prophets have gone out into the world. By this you know the Spirit of God: Every spirit that confesses that Jesus Christ has come in the flesh is of God, and every spirit that does not confess that Jesus Christ has come in the flesh is not of God. And this is the spirit of the Antichrist, which you have heard was coming, and is now already in the world".

Prophetic grace and utterances come during times of worship to create awareness, and address issues in people's lives. They deal with issues of the past, present, and future circumstances people face in life. There are different forms of prophetic grace and utterances during worship. This gifting swings into action when there is a demand, a hunger to hear from God, and an expectation in the heart of the people. In Psalm chapter 107:20 (NLT) the scripture says,

"He sent out his word and healed them and delivered them from their destruction".

This is because the people cried out to God in the first place.

Below are a few other ways Prophetic Grace and Utterance can manifest during worship:

1. Faith-building Prophecy

This comes when faith-building prophecy is released to confirm the spoken word of God. It encourages one to hold on to God until His appointed time. In Numbers 23:19 (NLT), the bible says,

*"**God is not a man, that he should lie; neither the son of man, that he should repent: hath he said, and shall he not do it? or hath he spoken, and shall he not make it good?**"*

2. Word of Warning Prophecy

Word of warning prophecy is given to create an awareness of unexpected danger and to proffer solutions for safety. This may also come with instructions on how to deal with the situation at hand and how to address it in the future.

3. Corrective Prophecy

Corrective prophecy serves as a reminder to man to reverently fear God. The man by nature easily forgets things, so they fall back into doing what they have been warned against in the past. The entire book of Judges typifies this point, and it was like a roller-coaster. When the children of Israel in sin disobeyed God, He would allow their enemies to deal with them for a while and then they would cry to God, and He would forgive their sins. Not so long after He forgave them, they had dived right back into the ocean of sin and the cycle continued.

The irony about corrective prophecy is that it can swing both ways. The correction can be for the prophet or for the people. God said to Prophet Ezekiel in Ezekiel 3:18 (NKJV):

"When I say to the wicked, 'You shall surely die,' and you give him no warning, nor speak to warn the wicked from his wicked way, to save his life, that same wicked man shall die in his iniquity; but his blood I will require at your hand."

The danger for the worshipper on corrective prophecy is that you cannot disobey God or be judgmental about who you are sent to because there will be consequences. The book of Jonah 1: 1– 3 (NKJV) reads:

"Now the word of the Lord came to Jonah the son of Amittai, saying, "Arise, go to Nineveh, that great city, and cry out against it; for their wickedness has come up before Me." But Jonah arose to flee to Tarshish from the presence of the Lord. He went down to Joppa, and found a ship going to Tarshish; so, he paid the fare, and went down into it, to go with them to Tarshish from the presence of the Lord."

How could he have ever thought of pulling this escapade through? The God of the universe, who knows and sees, and you chose to run away from His presence because you did not like His stand on an issue important to Him. It was the most stupid decision anyone could have made and after he found himself in the belly of the fish, he returned to his senses and eventually went to Nineveh in Jonah 3:2– 5 (NKJV) after God had to speak to him about it again:

"Arise, go to Nineveh, that great city, and preach to it the message that I tell you." So Jonah arose and went to Nineveh, according to the word of the Lord. Now Nineveh was an exceedingly great

city, a three-day journey in extent. And Jonah began to enter the city on the first day's walk. Then he cried out and said, "Yet forty days, and Nineveh shall be overthrown!" So the people of Nineveh believed God, proclaimed a fast, and put on sackcloth, from the greatest to the least of them."

All that God needs from a sinner is repentance and Proverbs 28:13 (NKJV), tells us: *"He who covers his sins will not prosper, But whoever confesses and forsakes them will have mercy."*
This was exactly what the people of Nineveh had to do. In deep repentance, they believed God, proclaimed a fast, and put on sackcloth, from the greatest to the least of them and God showed them mercy (Jon 3:10).

4. Word of Deliverance Prophecy
The words of deliverance prophecy unravel hurt, rejection, offense, and sickness, and it comes with solutions to the issues at hand through healing and restoration of the afflicted souls. In Exodus 3:7 - 10 (NKJV) we read:

"And the Lord said: "I have surely seen the oppression of My people who are in Egypt and have heard their cry because of their task-masters, for I know their sorrows. So I have come down to deliver them out of the hand of the Egyptians, and to bring them up from that land to a good and large land, to a land flowing with milk and honey, to the place of the Canaanites and the Hittites and the Amorites and the Perizzites and the Hivites and the Jebusites. Now therefore, behold, the cry of the children of Israel has come to Me, and I have also seen the oppression with which the Egyptians oppress them. Come now, therefore, and I will send you to Pharaoh that you may bring My people, the children of Israel, out of Egypt."

B. Power of Worship in the Times of Crisis

God needed a man to carry out the assignment and the lot fell on Moses. It was a tough assignment but after ten plagues and many destructions with the death of the firstborns in Egypt, Pharaoh let them go and Israel was delivered from bondage.

The power of Worship in times of crisis is beyond human reasoning or logic. The fact of the matter is, what has singing, clapping, dancing, jumping, and a host of other things got to do with worship? It is the only means we know to express our gratitude to God in times of crisis. Humanly speaking, turn around in crisis might seem impossible but not with God as Luke 1:37 (NKJV) emphatically tells us: "*With man it is impossible, but with God nothing shall be impossible*". The same was repeated in Mark chapter 10:27.

For example, the historical account of Israel and the wall of Jericho I worthy of mention here. From the description we read about the thickness of walls, it is deduced that between five to six cars could drive safely on one wing of it, side by side with no friction. This is a picture of unarguable impenetrable impossibility, yet worship brought the walls down. The summary of this event is seen in Joshua 6: 1– 16 (NKJV), which is quoted in part here:

"Now Jericho was securely shut up because of the children of Israel; none went out, and none came in.
Now Joshua had commanded the people, saying, "You shall not shout or make any noise with your voice, nor shall a word proceed out of your mouth, until the day I say to you, 'Shout!' Then you shall shout."

But it came to pass on the seventh day that they rose early, about the dawning of the day, and marched around the city seven times in the same manner. On that day only they marched around the city seven times. And the seventh time it happened, when the priests blew the trumpets, that Joshua said to the people: "Shout, for the Lord has given you the city. So the people shouted when the priests blew the trumpets. And it happened when the people heard the sound of the trumpet, and the people shouted with a great shout that the wall fell down..."
(Josh 6:1, 10, 15-16, 20 NKJV)

This is the evidence of what our God can do. In another instance, we read the account in 2 Chronicles 20:14--- 17 (NKJV):

"Then the Spirit of the Lord came upon Jahaziel the son of Zechariah, the son of Benaiah, the son of Jeiel, the son of Mattaniah, a Levite of the sons of Asaph, in the midst of the assembly. And he said, "Listen, all you of Judah and you inhabitants of Jerusalem, and you, King Jehoshaphat! Thus says the Lord to you: 'Do not be afraid nor dismayed because of this great multitude, for the battle is not yours, but God's. Tomorrow go down against them. They will surely come up by the Ascent of Ziz, and you will find them at the end of the [a]brook before the Wilderness of Jeruel. You will not need to fight in this battle. Position yourselves, stand still and see the salvation of the Lord, who is with you, O Judah and Jerusalem!' Do not fear or be dismayed; tomorrow go out against them, for the Lord is with you".

The question one may want to ask is:

"What has a King leading worship during an attack from three invading armies against Judah got to do with victory?"

It does not make sense, but King Jehoshaphat understood the power and importance of worship in crisis. He knew that his worship simply meant **"To you oh Lord I surrender. Outside of you Lord it is over."** King Jehoshaphat simply committed God to uphold His name.

I cannot over-emphasize the importance of one continuously inhabiting God's presence, nothing and I mean nothing, shall be able to withstand such a fellow. Because Psalm 91:1-11 tells us so. The verses quoted in parts 1 to 4 (NKJV) state:

"He who dwells in the secret place of the Most High Shall abide under the shadow of the Almighty. I will say of the Lord, "He is my refuge and my fortress; My God, in Him I will trust." Surely, He shall deliver you from the snare of the fowler And from the perilous pestilence. He shall cover you with His feathers, And under His wings you shall take refuge; His truth shall be your shield and buckler."

Furthermore, he assures us that the person shall not be afraid of the terror by night, the arrow that flies by day, the pestilence that walks in darkness, and the destruction that lay waste at noonday. This man is so secure in the Lord that no matter the levels of attack that come his way, they shall not come near him. He will only with his eyes see the reward of the wicked. This is because this person has made the Lord his refuge and his dwelling place. Therefore, no evil shall befall him neither shall any plague come near his dwelling. The Lord shall give His angels charge over and keep him in all his ways.

So, worship in a time of crisis is simply the act of handing over the crisis to the one who has the power to deal with it – the One who specializes in handling impossibilities. From the scripture above, we can see the confidence and resolute attitude of the one who enjoys God's presence. How well do you trust God, for you to hand over all your worries unto Him?

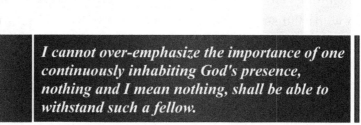

I cannot over-emphasize the importance of one continuously inhabiting God's presence, nothing and I mean nothing, shall be able to withstand such a fellow.

Understanding Worship

CHAPTER 4

Understanding Worship

Worship as we know it comes with a lot of myths and confusion that are neither true nor meaningful. Worship is way simpler to one whose whole being is in it for God and Him alone. In John 4:23—24 (NKJV) we read,

"But the hour is coming, and now is, when the true worshipers will worship the Father in spirit and truth; for the Father is seeking (desires) such to worship Him. God is Spirit, and those who worship Him must worship in spirit and truth".

God seeks meaning and He desires those who will worship Him as He needs to be worshipped. That is why worship must be done holistically, as every fiber of one's life must be involved. Worship cannot be done shabbily or with an ulterior motive.

Due to the reason of choice, worship becomes what you make it. In other words, who or what you choose to worship becomes your prerogative but that does not imply there will be no consequences. In Deuteronomy 4:24 (NKJV) we are told that:

"For the Lord your God is a consuming fire, a jealous God."

The question is why would God be jealous? We find the answer in Exodus 22:20 (NKJV) which says:

"He who sacrifices to any god, except to the Lord only, he shall be utterly destroyed."

The first and most important commandment given to Moses to the children of Israel was for them not to bow, sacrifice, or serve any other god except the God of Israel. The consequence of violating this commandment was death. Yet, almost everyone sees Him as a God of mercy forgetting that He is also a God of Principles. God upholds His word more than His name. In Psalm 138:2c (NKJV), we read:

"For You have magnified Your word above all Your name".

Whether you are a Christian or not, this principle applies to all, God is God regardless. The worship of Him is no different, there are rules and regulations on how to worship Him. We have and serve a very meticulous God who has created us for this singular purpose in life— to worship Him. Hence, how, where, and when we worship Him matters to Him in particular. This brings us to that point where some demystifying needs to be done by understanding some facts about worship. Let us review together below what Worship is NOT!

A. What Worship is Not

For some music, singing or worship is strictly a means to an end. But for the purpose of clarity, worship, music, or singing, in this book, is focused on a Church setting where it is to the glory of God, yet it must be done with all brilliance, professionalism, and excellence! Below are a few points of what worship is not:

1. Worship is not just Singing,

Singing is only a tool or one of many ways via which worship is conveyed. In effect, worship is not just singing a song, it is much more than that!

2. Worship is not a Feeling or an Emotion.

Feelings or emotions are temporal, they are transient, and they have to do with a person's mood. They flow with what is happening in one's life now. True Worship is not so. It is done with the right spirit, attitude, and in truth. God demands worship irrespective of whether you feel like it or not.

3. Worship cannot be Done with the Sole Aim of making Money.

Let us get some understanding here about money. Money is not evil; it is the love of money to the point where you are literally controlled by it that is evil. Money is needed to do the work of the Kingdom, but when money becomes the determining factor, something is fundamentally wrong.

We must understand that money chases after vision and purpose; because where there is a vision, there will be provision. God who gave you the vision knows your every need. So, if you serve Him wholeheartedly, money will come looking for you, because God is willing to meet your every need. He is a promise keeper and provider. David made it very clear in Psalm 23:1(NKJV) *"The Lord is my shepherd; I shall not want."*

4. Worship is Not about Fame.

The altar is not a stage for self-aggrandizement, rather it is a place of total reverence to God and humility before Him. When self-promotion is in the mix, pride is the foundation of this self-projection, but we must reject 'Mr. Flesh', and treat God with honor due to His name.

Therefore, "*Give unto the LORD, O ye mighty, give unto the LORD glory and strength. Give unto the LORD the glory due unto his name; Worship the LORD in the beauty of holiness.*" (Ps 29:1-2 NKJV)

5. Worship is Not about Competition.

We are not in a talent show or in a competition to see who the better worshipper of God is, yet we are expected to always come with our A-game. Worship is spiritual and no iota of the flesh must in any way be entertained. Even if the thought crosses your mind, reject it, and return all the glory to God. Effective and acceptable worship must be done in the beauty of holiness.

"*Therefore, I urge you, brothers and sisters, in view of God's mercy to offer your bodies as a living sacrifice, holy and pleasing to God – this is your true and proper worship.*" (Rom 12:1 NIV)

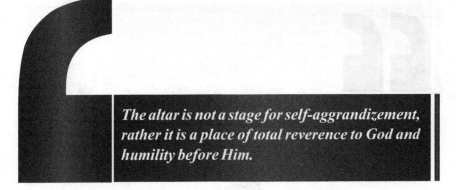

The altar is not a stage for self-aggrandizement, rather it is a place of total reverence to God and humility before Him.

Types Of Worship

CHAPTER 5

Types Of Worship

Background

In the previous chapter, we examined what worship is not, and in this chapter, we will review together the different types of worship. It is important you know that there is more than one word that means "Worship" in the Hebrew language. A word in Hebrew can mean more than one thing at a time, such a word for example is "Worship" which can also mean "Praise". Likewise, there are many gestures that mean worship or praising God in Hebrew. Gestures like singing, dancing, raising hands, clapping, bowing down, and extending one's arm.

Hence, these gestures represent the state of a worshipper's heart or mind during worship to God due to his or her personal life experience of God. Here are the types of worship or praise you will find both in the scriptures and in both individual and congregational worship today:

1. "Halal".
Halal means to shine, to be boastful, to glorify, to offer unrestrained praise. It involves jumping and dancing, with loud or clamorous sounds. The root for Halal means two things - Hallelujah, which is a combination of "praise" (Halal) and the name Yahweh.

We see a good example of this type of worship when King David brought in the Ark of the Lord from the house of Obed-Edom to the City of David in 2 Samuel 6:12-15!

"Now it was told King David, saying, "The Lord has blessed the house of Obed-Edom and all that belongs to him, because of the ark of God." So David went and brought up the ark of God from the house of Obed-Edom to the City of David with gladness. And so it was, when those bearing the ark of the Lord had gone six paces, that he sacrificed oxen and fatted sheep. Then David danced before the Lord with all his might; and David was wearing a linen ephod. So David and all the house of Israel brought up the ark of the Lord with shouting and with the sound of the trumpet." (2 Sam 6:12-15 NKJV)

"Praise (Hallelujah) ye the Lord, praise (Hallelujah) o ye servants of the Lord, praise (Hallelujah) the name of the Lord." (Ps 113:1 NKJV)

2. "Tehilah":
Tehilah means to spontaneously sing and praise God from your spirit with unrehearsed songs. It means to bring light and celebration with songs, shouts, and holy noise.

"But thou art holy, O thou that inhabitest the praises (Tehilah) of Israel". (Ps 22:3 KJV)

3. "Zamar"
Zamar implies praising God with string instruments. It is the idea of making music by plucking at strings with fingers and singing praises unto God.

"Shout joyfully to the Lord, all the earth; Break forth in song, rejoice, and sing praises." (Ps 98:4 NKJV)

4. "Yadah".

To Yadah means to praise God with your hand (yad). It means to throw your hands up and forward while making a confession about God.

"O Lord, You are my God. I will exalt You, I will praise Your name, For You have done wonderful things; Your counsels of old are faithfulness and truth." (Is 25:1 KJV)

"And so it was, when Moses held up his hand, that Israel prevailed; and when he let down his hand, Amalek prevailed. But Moses' hands became heavy; so they took a stone and put it under him, and he sat on it. And Aaron and Hur supported his hands, one on one side, and the other on the other side; and his hands were steady until the going down of the sun." *(Ex 17:11-12 NKJV)*

"And I, if I am lifted up from the earth, will draw all peoples to Myself." (Jn 12:32 NKJV)

5. "Towdah"

Towdah is another type of praise to God. It's to lift your hands in thanksgiving to God for His lovingkindness. We extend our hands in total adoration to God in surrendered worship.

"Let them sacrifice the sacrifices of thanksgiving And declare His works with rejoicing." (Ps 107:22 NKJV)

6. "Barack".

Barack is the desire to worship or praise God in reverence, in the absolute knowledge of Him, and in a posture that is not comfortable.

It is an act of abandoning physical comfort in passionate humility to express one's praises and worship to God Almighty. The act of kneeling in reverence and submission to God. *"Blessed be God, Who has not turned away my prayer, Nor His mercy from me!"* (Psalm 66:20 NKJV)

"So Ahab went up to eat and drink. And Elijah went up to the top of Carmel; then he bowed down on the ground, and put his face between his knees." (1 Kings 18:42 NKJV)

7. "Shabach".

Shabach means to praise God aloud, give a joyous shout of testimony, and loud adoration to Him. It means to proclaim unashamed, the glory, triumph, power, mercy, and love of God. Shabach is not just being loud, rather it entails the expression of our whole being totally uninhibited.

"Praise the Lord, all you Gentiles! Laud Him, all you peoples!" (Ps 117:1 NKJV)

"Because Your lovingkindness is better than life, My lips shall praise You. Thus I will bless You while I live; I will lift up my hands in Your name." (Ps 63:3-4 NKJV)

"One generation shall praise Your works to another, And shall declare Your mighty acts." (Ps 145:4 NKJV)

In conclusion, apart from our Lord Jesus Christ, the only other person who pleased God deeply in worship was King Solomon.

God was so pleased with him because he was doing basically what Jesus asked each one of us to do as found in the book of Matthew 6:33:

"Seek first the kingdom of God and his righteousness." (NKJV)

Solomon was seeking not his own pleasure and power but God's pleasure. The lifestyle of worship for a true believer or a Christian can never be over emphasized because of its importance. Worship is everything to God so it should also be for you and me. Do all you can to be a true worshipper of God and be blessed!

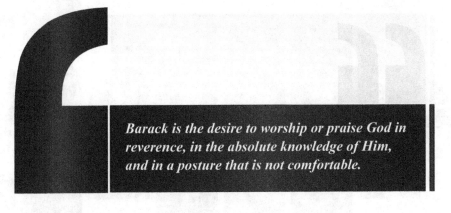

Barack is the desire to worship or praise God in reverence, in the absolute knowledge of Him, and in a posture that is not comfortable.

The Choir

CHAPTER 6

The Choir

"Indeed it came to pass, when the trumpeters and singers were as one, to make one sound to be heard in praising and thanking the Lord, and when they lifted up their voice with the trumpets and cymbals and instruments of music, and praised the Lord, saying: "For He is good, For His mercy endures forever," that the house, the house of the Lord, was filled with a cloud so that the priests could not continue ministering because of the cloud; for the glory of the Lord filled the house of God." (2 Chron 5:13-14 NKJV)

The Choir came into full display in the Bible during King David's reign in Israel. He gave more structure for the priestly family (Aaron Family) and broke them into various groups for different functions in the tabernacle. It is highly imperative that every Pastor or church leader must understand the importance of music, worship, and Choir in their local church. They must have a flair for music and do everything in their capacity to aid their Choir for a great result. This is the mind of God because Judah (Praise) must always lead the tribes in worship.

To bring down the glory of God, we need the Choir to lead us in offering high praises to Him.

The Choir primes the service for every activity to be done during this time. The service should have oil of the anointing to thrive which includes the prayer session and the word. They prepare the ground for the seed of the word to be planted by the pastor, and the hearts of the people are open to change or transformation, and the unbelievers are also made ready to receive Jesus as their Lord and Saviour.

A. What is a Choir?

1. A Choir can be Defined as:
a) An organized company of *singers*
b) A group of instruments of the same class
c) The part of a cathedral or large church between the high altar and the nave, used by the Choir and clergy.

The definitions above are all from the Web Dictionary. In actual sense, a Choir is way deeper than these definitions. Yes, any group of people can decide to set up a Choir, but for the purpose of this book, we are talking about a Christian Choir, a Spiritual and Christ-centered Choir. A Choir therefore can be defined as: **"a group of individuals who have identified the fact that they have a calling as Christians to worship or sing songs strictly to the glory of God."**

They have also decided to submit such desires and gifts to authority in the person of a Pastor or Church Leader and would adhere to every instruction given by the pastor or leader. This is how total submission to authority is developed in the Choir and in the body of Christ.

2. Choir Director or Leader
A fully functioning Choir should have a Choir Director or at the least a Choir leader who shepherds them in prayers, rehearsals, and cares for their total personal well-being.

He or she oversees the selection of songs, and hymns appropriate for each of the services, programs, or conferences.

He or she should be able to write or encourage those gifted in the Choir to prayerfully bring forth new songs from the throne of grace. This leader or sub-leader reports to the Minister-in-Charge or the Senior Pastor as the case may be.

B. The Functioning Choir

1. Expectations:

Gone are the days a Pastor or a church leader will downplay the role of the Choir in a church or in any setting where music is needed to further enhance the work of the Kingdom.

It is highly recommended that much attention be paid to building a Choir that gives her congregation a reason to return to church every week. All church Pastors and leaders are encouraged to take a survey of their services and ask the people what brings them to church weekly.

In my local church, we found out after taking such a survey, that the first three reasons why people came back to church every given Wednesday and Sunday were:
a) The Love shown by the leadership and brethren
b) The Word of Life preached
c) The Praise and Worship Sessions (Choir/Music)

It has been like this in my local church for over seven years of my presence and ministry there. Whether you want to believe it or not, Pastors, and church leaders, please understand that we have people who come to church solely because of the Choir, and the music they minister, and they are wholeheartedly satisfied by it. Please do not make the mistake of frustrating your worship team or Choir members, because it will affect the services and your congregation.

I am of the school of thought that believes you should pay A-List singers and musicians or else another would do so by attracting them with mouth-watering offers!

2. Why your Gifted Choir Members should be Paid

a) It is scriptural that the whole tribe of the children of Israel who served God in this capacity were made to dedicate their lives to God in full without distractions. They were led by the family of Aaron and all the other tribes contributed to their well-being. God was their inheritance.

b) When they are well renumerated, they are in the church's employment, and this makes them have a 9 to 5 job. Can you imagine a Choir or worship team given solely to practicing, and writing worship and praise songs, without the worry of where their next food will come from or how to pay their bills? Compare this with another team, where they are hardly committed to a church. Rather, they are hired on a secular job, and are out there working, but share part of their time with the church as they deem fit.

The danger here is that if they are duly committed to their job and an overtime schedule opens for them, they will surely go for it. If this person plays a key role in the Choir, his absence will automatically cause disruption in the service that day. From the scenario painted you will realize that the final Choir production will be different, the spirit behind each work will speak for itself.

c) You have a committed and stable worship band and Choir. A team that is not visibly stressed during services, having spent the better part of their energy at their secular jobs.

This team is well-focused and thoroughly connected with the throne of Grace in spirit and in truth. A new song easily flows from such hearts and minds, totally dedicated to God.

C. The Role of the Choir in Church

1. They are to serve the "Head Pastor" of the church. In Numbers 3:5-6 (NKJV) we read:

> *"And the Lord spoke to Moses, saying: "Bring the tribe of Levi near, and present them before Aaron the priest, that they may serve him."*

In serving the Pastor, the Choir must meet with him or her as often as possible. This way there is a connection between the Pastor and the Choir. The term "**Catching the spirit of the pastor happens during these meetings**", because this is where they get to really know their Pastor's mind and personality.

2. They are to Meet the need of the people.
> *"And they shall attend to his needs and the needs of the whole congregation before the tabernacle of meeting, to do the work of the tabernacle."* (Num. 3:7 NKJV)

On average per week, people come to church for various reasons. There are a percentage of the people who come in squarely for the worship. During this time all their issues are met simply because their faith is anchored to it. They still get blessed by other things, but music had done it for them. Pastors and church leaders must feed these aspects by investing in the music ministry, hire professionals and let them help groom children born in the church who have flair for music. Years to come there will be a great difference as those children grow to fill into those worship spaces for the church.

3. They Make sure that the right atmosphere is created in the Church.

"Also they shall attend to all the furnishings of the tabernacle of meeting, and to the needs of the children of Israel, to do the work of the tabernacle." (Num. 3:8 NKJV).

This is a very important point. The essence of having a Choir is to create an atmosphere where everywhere is charged and when the pastor comes on the pulpit, he or she simply flows easily into the Word, and if well done, he or she will hardly look at his or her notes. Why? Because of the presence of God. This is purely achievable by the level of preparedness put in by the Choir.

D. A few Questions for the Choir

I have a few questions for the Choir:

1. How often do you as a team fast and pray in a week?

2. How often do you study the Word?

3. How is your personal life outside the church?

If you say worship is a lifestyle, there must not be a difference between what we see at church, and what we see at home, or in the public.

4. How hungry are you for God, and for the manifestation of His power, during your Choir ministrations?

The genuine answers given to the above questions will launch any Choir into that space of dwelling perpetually in God's presence. Psalm 91:1 (NKJV), says: *"He who dwells in the secret place of the Most High Shall abide under the shadow of the Almighty."*

The right atmosphere is achieved by dwelling in His presence, continually in prayers, the study of His Word, and putting to practice what you have learned. God's presence exudes "Fullness", and that fullness radiates and is catchy too!

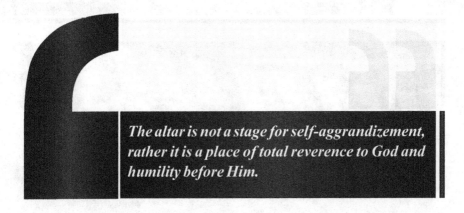

> *The altar is not a stage for self-aggrandizement, rather it is a place of total reverence to God and humility before Him.*

Warning About Having a Choir

CHAPTER

7

Background Tips

When raising a Choir, it is important to always remember that a Choir is made up of a group of people who have identified their gifts and calling and have decided to submit them to authority. In a nutshell, they are humans prone to make mistakes, and can take a wrong turn in life and for this reason the watchwords while dealing with them are love and compassion.

To Pastors and church leaders, please give room for the process to birth maturity as this will differ in individuals. That does not in any way stop you from telling each other the truth especially when it hurts, but allow love to guard your delivery and choice of words.

Human levels of maturity differ, but it is the responsibility of the Pastor or church leader to show the Choir what is expected of them. This is not to be done just once but it must be a continuous process until it is understood by the Choir. Just as it is expected to recast the vision of the church to the body, you need to let the Choir know the visionary's expectations you have for them as you carry them along.

Having laid bare, the background for this chapter, please examine carefully, the thoughts below as you plan to raise a Choir or if you already have one raised.

1.Not everybody can be in a Choir

Due to the demand and the prestige that comes with being in a Choir, it can be very dangerous if you lack the right character. For some reason, everybody believes they can sing. This is very true, but does everybody have the spiritual discipline, temperament, and diligence required to be in a Choir? For this reason, it is not true that everybody can sing in a spirit-filled Christian Choir!

The Choir's assignment in the church is deeply spiritual, and this is a major consideration, not the Choir member's voices. On the relevance of a Choir member's voice please be aware that a bathroom voice is totally different from the actual singing voice. You need to be mature enough to know that there is much more work to be done on your vocals than meets the eye. I am sure you are aware that your tongue has a connection with your heart. Therefore a heart full of pride, desiring public visibility, and showing off as a reason for being in the Choir, is not a feasible option and is a disaster waiting to happen.

What then should the leadership be looking for in a Choir audition? The required qualities to look for are spiritual discipline, the person's prayer life, the ability to fast, spending time in the Word, and showing integrity of character. Full details of these qualities would be gleaned down the road as relationships are built. Life is in phases and stages, if you as a person want to join the Choir, it is your responsibility to know where you are when taking decisions that best suit that stage of your life. For example, a nursing mother needs time off to take care of herself, her baby, and her family without feeling guilty or sad. Yes, such a person will be missed in the Choir but her first ministry in this instance is her family. **James 3:1-2** (NKJV) **says:**

"My brethren, let not many of you become teachers, knowing that we shall receive a stricter judgment. For we all stumble in many things. If anyone does not stumble in word, he is a perfect man, able also to bridle the whole body".

In other words, saying "No" can just be a way of saving lives. Not everyone can be in the Choir to sing depending on how large or big the Choir is. If the vision of the Pastor is to have a mass Choir, a lot of people will be required but from experience, not all of them will be qualified to sing.

Now because you are dealing with people (volunteers at that), you need to be wise and strategic in engaging them. You will need to make use of the strategy of King David before setting up a Choir.

2. King David's Strategic Approach
Before King David introduced a more administrative structure to the Choir in Israel, the Choir or organized worshipping of God was headed by the family of Aaron. For example, in Numbers 4:1-15, God instructed Moses to consecrate Aaron and his family to become the head priest of worship and they were to carry out the following:

i) Take a census of the Levite clan of Kohath by subclans and families and register all the men between the ages of thirty and fifty who were qualified to work in the Tent of the LORD's presence. Their service was most holy.

ii)   When it was time to break camp, Aaron and his sons were to enter the Tent, take down the curtain in front of the Covenant Box, and cover the Box with it.

iii)   To put a fine leather cover over it, spread a cloth of solid blue on top, and then insert the carrying poles.

iv)   Spread a blue cloth over the table for the bread offered to the LORD and put on it the dishes, the incense bowls, the offering bowls, and the jars for the wine offering.

v)   There would always be bread on the table.

vi)   Spread red cloth over all of this, put a fine leather cover over it, and then insert the carrying poles.

vii)   Take a blue cloth and cover the lampstand, with its lamps, tongs, trays, and all the olive oil containers.

viii)   Wrap it and all its equipment in a fine leather cover and place it on a carrying frame.

ix)   Next, they spread a blue cloth over the gold altar, put a fine leather cover over it, and then insert the carrying poles.

x)   Take all the utensils used in the Holy Place, wrap them in a blue cloth, put a fine leather cover over them, and place them on a carrying frame.

xi)   Remove the greasy ashes from the altar and spread a purple cloth over it.

xii)   Put on it all the equipment used in the service at the altar: fire pans, hooks, shovels, and basins.

xiii)   They were to put a fine leather cover over it and insert the carrying poles.

xiv) When it was time to break camp, the clan of Kohath would carry the sacred objects only after Aaron and his sons had finished covering them and all their equipment.

xv)   The Kohath clan were not allowed to touch the sacred objects, or they would die."

3. The Example from the Bible

Aaron and his sons further broke down the duties of the children of Levi by dividing them into four clans and given them delegated responsibilities.

The four groups are:
1. Aaron and his sons
2. The Kohathites
3. The Gershonites, and
4. The Merarites

1. Aaron and his sons

The duties of Aaron and his sons were to lead the clans in fulfilling their duties in the temple as seen in the scriptures above in Numbers 4:1- 15.

2. The Kohathites

Now the duty and responsibilities of the Kohath clan were to do the followings whenever the Tent is moved.

a) They are to dismantle the Holy place.

b) They are to pack the vessels and the instruments used in the Holy place, and no other Levite was allowed to even touch anything used in this chamber. If they did, they would die. These responsibilities were set out in the book of Numbers 4:15, 18 - 20.

"And when Aaron and his sons have finished covering the sanctuary and all the furnishings of the sanctuary when the camp is set to go, then the sons of Kohath shall come to carry them; but they shall not touch any holy thing, lest they die. "These are the things in the tabernacle of meeting which the sons of Kohath are to carry."

"Do not cut off the tribe of the families of the Kohathites from among the Levites; but do this in regard to them, that they may live and not die when they approach the most holy things: Aaron and his sons shall go in and appoint each of them to his service and his task. But they shall not go in to watch while the holy things are being covered, lest they die."
(Num. 4:15, 18 – 20 NKJV)

This further explains why Uzzah was killed when he tried to steady the **"cart"** when the Ark of God was almost falling in 2 Samuel 6: 6 – 7 (NKJV):

"And when they came to Nachon's threshing floor, Uzzah put out his hand to the ark of God and took hold of it, for the oxen stumbled. Then the anger of the Lord was aroused against Uzzah, and God struck him there for his error; and he died there by the ark of God."

The great error was that the Ark of God was to be carried on the shoulders of men, rather the Ark was laid on a new cart pulled by cattle. God had specifically told Moses that the Kohathites were to bear it **on their shoulders,** according to the Word of the Lord to him in Numbers 7: 9 (KJV).

"But unto the sons of Kohath, he gave none: because the service of the sanctuary belonging unto them [was that] they should bear upon their shoulders." (Num. 7:9 NKJV).

Not everybody is allowed in the Choir because it is not everybody that is disciplined to follow laid down rules, and as we see in the case of Uzzah there is danger in not following instructions. To be in the Choir, one must be trained to do the right thing. However, the person to be trained must be willing and obedient to adhere to rules and regulations. He or she must submit to authority to thrive. For example, the Kohathites' duties or responsibilities were to:

i) Oversee the bearing of The Ark of the Covenant.
ii) Oversee the Vessels packed by Aaron and his sons

Now the other families Gershonites and Merarites of the Tribe of Levi could carry their items on Wagons and Oxen (Numbers 7:6-8 KJV): *"And Moses took the wagons and the oxen and gave them unto the Levites. Two wagons and four oxen he gave unto the sons of Gershon, according to their service; And four wagons and eight oxen he gave unto the sons of Merari, according unto their service, under the hand of Ithamar the son of Aaron the priest."*

3. The Gershonites
The responsibilities of the Gershonites were to oversee the followings:

a) The Services in the Tabernacle of the congregation.
b) The Bearing of the curtains, the badger skins, and instruments.
c) They were to be under the supervision of Ithamar, Aaron's son, as stated in Numbers 4:28 (AMP).

"This [is] the service of the families of the sons of Gershon in the tabernacle of the congregation: and their charge [shall be] under the hand of Ithamar the son of Aaron the priest."

4. The Merarites

The responsibilities of the Merarites were to oversee the followings:

a) Provide services in the Tabernacle of the Congregation.

b) And in charge of boards, bars. Pillars sockets pins cords instruments etc.

They were under the supervision of Ithamar. As seen in Numbers 4:29 - 33 (NKJV),

"As for the sons of Merari, you shall number them by their families and by their fathers' house. From thirty years old and above, even to fifty years old, you shall number them, everyone who enters the service to do the work of the tabernacle of meeting. And this is what they must carry as all their service for the tabernacle of meeting: the boards of the tabernacle, its bars, its pillars, its sockets, and the pillars around the court with their sockets, pegs, and cords, with all their furnishings and all their service; and you shall assign to each man by name the items he must carry. This is the service of the families of the sons of Merari, as all their service for the tabernacle of meeting, under the [a]authority of Ithamar the son of Aaron the priest."

The Levites did not choose to do what pleased them, they were under God's ordained leadership supervision as seen in Numbers chapter 4:19 - 20 (NKJV). *"but do this in regard to them, that they may live and not die when they approach the most holy things: Aaron and his sons shall go in and appoint each of them to his service and his task. But they shall not go in to watch while the holy things are being covered, lest they die."*

Not all the Levites served in the same office or do the same job. To adhere to standards their job specifications are clearly spelled out as well as the duties to be carried out. They also maintained different and specific positions in the journey and when they are encamped. The individual position of each tribe is itemized below:

i) Kohathites – always encamped on the South side of the tabernacle.

ii) Gershonites – Occupy the Western side.

iii) Merarites – take their position on the Northern side.

iv) Moses, Aaron, and Aaron's Sons - occupy the Eastern side.

This organized structure of service in the Tabernacle of the Congregation continued but was modified by King David when he took over rulership from King Saul. So during King David's reign, some changes were introduced. You will find these changes in 1 Chronicles 23:24 – 27 (NKJV):

"These were the sons of Levi by their fathers' houses—the heads of the fathers' houses as they were counted individually by the number of their names, who did the work for the service of the house of the LORD, from the age of twenty years and above. For David said, "The LORD God of Israel has given rest to His people, that they may dwell in Jerusalem forever"; and also to the Levites, "They shall no longer carry the tabernacle or any of the articles for its service." For by the last words of David the Levites were numbered from twenty years old and above."

The first change we see is that all Levites were registered for service when they reached the age of twenty.

After the census of the descendant of Levi was done at the order of King David, he introduced new structure and broke down their duties even further. Please find below the changes made:

1. He employed the services of Song leaders and skilled musicians to conduct worship services. (1 Chron 6:31-33, 39; 25:1-7).
2. New appointments were made in the service of the House of the Lord. (1 Chron 6:48).

3. Gatekeepers/Ushers were appointed. (1 Chron 9:17-24).

4. Trustees or their equivalents were appointed. (1 Chron 9:26-31)

5. Treasuries and treasurers were also set up (1 Chron 9:26; 26:20-28)

When Jesus Christ came on the scene in the New Testament, He did not make any changes to these offices. They remained as a foreshadowing from the Old Testament (John 4:23-24). Not everybody sang at the same time but for mass Choir's sake, everybody can come together during a major event and sing together but the A-list singers will handle the microphones.

C. Word of Caution

1. Character: Pride can easily set in

a) There is a very thin line between humility and pride, and most do not realize when it is crossed. The reason the flesh can sing now in the Choir is that one fellow did not realize that he had crossed the line and that was the devil who used to be the chief angel, a walking sound bag. Brethren, from personal experience it is a very thin line.

If you are a guy, ladies offer themselves with ease to you, and vice versa. Yes, it is very real.

The book of Proverbs 16:18 (KJV) says, ***"Pride goes before destruction, a haughty spirit before a fall."*** The most painful part of this point is that the defaulting party hardly knows they have gone astray.

b) Money is another killer, if you have no control, it will control you, destroy you and afterward fly away.

c) If not well looked after, family is another thin line to watch out for. There must be a proper balance – communication must be on point always. You cannot afford to forget anything.

2. Lifestyle (Holiness, Sexual Purity, etc.) (Leviticus 18)

As painful as this point is, I must mention it because the Choir is also of the most troubled parts of the body of Christ. The attack on these groups of people is unimaginable. From spiritual to physical, and mental. The list goes on, but the most prevailing attack on the Choir is a sexual attack. The devil knows that God cannot behold iniquity, so this attack becomes its most potent weapon against it. In Habakkuk 1:13 (NKJV), we read.

> *"You are of purer eyes than to behold evil, And cannot look on wickedness. Why do You look on those who deal treacherously, And hold Your tongue when the wicked devours A person more righteous than he?"*

I am not saying there are no other forms of attack or weaknesses, but sexual lust has always been his modus operandi. Hence, the onus lies on everyone to know themselves, and know their strengths and weaknesses. They should actively pray and take practical measures not to fall prey to the whiles of the enemy.

The reason for this is that there is no excuse for any form of sin. In the book of Hebrews 13:4 (NKJV), we read:

"Marriage is honorable among all, and the bed undefiled; but fornicators and adulterers God will judge."

Any form of impurity will be judged and serving in the Choir always demands deep spiritual levels. So be careful as you watch and pray!

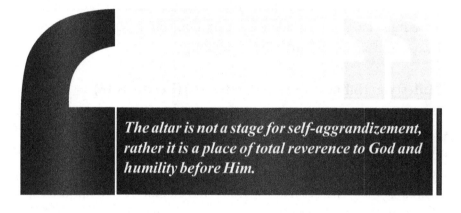

The altar is not a stage for self-aggrandizement, rather it is a place of total reverence to God and humility before Him.

Characteristics Of A Good Choir

CHAPTER 8

Introduction

In this chapter, I will be talking about some peculiar indications that will represent the special quality or identity that will be required to become a member of a Choir. These qualities will be the distinguishing factor(s) that will help a church or any organization that wants to have a musical plan added to its goals. Some of the distinguishing qualities are:

- A people submitted to authority, even when it seems not good or right. It's all about God's will for them (Elijah, Elisha, John the Revelator, etc.)
- A people deeply loyal to constituted authority and willing to obey without asking questions - (Moses, Joshua, and Paul, etc.).
- A people who in their character are reliable, dependable, consistent, trustworthy, and accountable both to the Leadership and others they work with.

A. What does it mean to submit to authority and how easy is it for one to submit?

1. Submission to Authority:

To Submit means: "**to give over or yield to the power or authority of another**." In Ephesians 5:21 (NKJV) we read "*Submitting to one another in the fear of God.*"

What this verse of scripture is not saying is that we submit to man, rather we are to submit to the God that man represents. It is in the submission that the grooming, learning, and training come.

2. Submitting to authority breeds Loyalty.

If this process is not properly done, there will be a crack in the wall. The submission that is been spoken of here is not based on choice or feeling, rather it is based on obeying God. Romans 13:1 to 3 (NIV) says,

"Let everyone be subject to the governing authorities, for there is no authority except that which God has established. The authorities that exist have been established by God. Consequently, whoever rebels against the authority is rebelling against what God has instituted, and those who do so will bring judgment on themselves. For rulers hold no terror for those who do right, but for those who do wrong. Do you want to be free from fear of the one in authority? Then do what is right and you will be commended."

The interesting thing about this passage of scripture is that we are made to know that every established authority is of God. Therefore anyone who rebels against such authority is rebelling against God, and consequently, will face judgment.

Those in authority are not there to punish those who do the right things but for those who do wrong. So, to be free from the fear of authority it is better to seek to do the right things.

Further down the passage in verse 4, Apostle Paul hinted at the fact that the person in authority is a servant of God for your good. *"They are God's servants, agents of wrath to bring punishment on the wrongdoer."* (V4 NIV).

With the argument advanced, it is necessary to submit to authorities *"...not only because of possible punishment but also as a matter of conscience."* (V5 NIV). These men in authority give their full time to govern and maintain order in society, and that is the reason we pay taxes as well (v6). Submitting to authority is so dear to God that any violation attracts serious punishment. Our God demands obedience to the words of constituted authority.

Elijah and Elisha are good examples for the Choir to follow on this topic. Once you know you are called into this ministry of Worship, you need help, and you need an authority in this field to submit to. 1 Kings 19:19 - 21 (NKJV) reads,

"So Elijah went from there and found Elisha son of Shaphat. He was ploughing with twelve yoke of oxen, and he himself was driving the twelfth pair. Elijah went up to him and threw his cloak around him. Elisha then left his oxen and ran after Elijah. "Let me kiss my father and mother goodbye," he said, "and then I will come with you." "Go back," Elijah replied. "What have I done to you?" So Elisha left him and went back. He took his yoke of oxen and slaughtered them. He burned the ploughing equipment to cook the meat and gave it to the people, and they ate. Then he set out to follow Elijah and became his servant."

Dear Choir, please understand that those leaders are not our friends or peers. In fact, when you meet real leaders, they are not pleasant at all, and they are not babysitters either. They are leaders because they have been chosen by God to represent Him. And if a leader is not doing well, it is not in our place to challenge his or her authority, rather we are to first pray about the matter and report to a higher authority concerning such a leader.

A.What does it mean to be Loyal?

1. Loyalty:

The word Loyal means; "...**to be dedicated, reliable, steadfast in allegiance or duty. It means to be unwavering in devotion to a friend or a vow, fanatically patriotic about a thing or a nation.**"

Loyalty is not an emotional thing - it is way more spiritual because it is borne out of commitment to someone or something. Therefore, when we talk about being loyal to authority it is a very deep thing. Therefore, one's loyalty must first be to God then He will lead you to whom you are to submit to, however not in eyeservice or men-pleasing!

As mentioned earlier, true loyalty draws strength from spirituality. You, without been told, willingly and freely uphold in prayer the one you submit to. That is why Apostle Paul encouraged Timothy and the body of Christ in 1 Timothy 2:1 - 2 (NIV),

"I urge, then, first of all, that petitions, prayers, intercession and thanksgiving be made for all people— for kings and all those in authority, that we may live peaceful and quiet lives in all godliness and holiness."

2. Loyalty is very important.

Loyalty, like submission is very important and crucial in every Choir. If there is any form of doubt of any sort, I always encourage people to speak up. In that way things are addressed, and not left to fester because if left to do so it will create animosity within the group. This can lead to self-doubt or doubt on the leadership side, and with that friction, one can stop receiving from either the leader or from the Choir. Such was the case of Gehazi as seen in the book of 2 Kings 5:20 to 27 (NIV) which is quoted in part.

> "*Gehazi, the servant of Elisha the man of God, said to himself, "My master was too easy on Naaman, this Aramean, by not accepting from him what he brought. As surely as the LORD lives, I will run after him and get something from him." So Gehazi hurried after Naaman. When Naaman saw him running toward him, he got down from the chariot to meet him. "Is everything all right?" he asked. "Everything is all right," Gehazi answered. "My master sent me to say, 'Two young men from the company of the prophets have just come to me from the hill country of Ephraim. Please give them a talent of silver and two sets of clothing.'" "By all means, take two talents," said Naaman. He urged Gehazi to accept them, and then tied up the two talents of silver in two bags, with two sets of clothing. He gave them to two of his servants, and they carried them ahead of Gehazi. When Gehazi came to the hill, he took the things from the servants and put them away in the house. He sent the men away and they left.*"
> (2 Kings 5:20 – 24 NIV).

The action of Gehazi here was very disloyal to God and his master. He lied, using his master's name to amass ill-gotten wealth, and later paid dearly for it.

Having collected his loot, he returned to stand before his master on spiritual ground doing as if nothing happened.

Sometimes, those who are close to spiritual power take it for granted. Here was Elisha with the double portion anointing of Elijah on him, should not this alone make Gehazi to fear? The truth is those who are on the path to perishing, do not listen to the voice of caution or wisdom. He had the opportunity to repent when his master asked him *"Where have you been, Gehazi?"* (v25 NIV). He lied *"Your servant didn't go anywhere," Gehazi answered."* *"But Elisha said to him, "Was not my spirit with you when the man got down from his chariot to meet you? Is this the time to take money or to accept clothes—or olive groves and vineyards, or flocks and herds, or male and female slaves? Naaman's leprosy will cling to you and to your descendants forever." Then Gehazi went from Elisha's presence and his skin was leprous—it had become as white as snow."* (vs. 26-27 NIV)

Disloyalty is a path to self-destruction, and when anyone walks this road he will lie, steal, or covet and engage in immorality with the opposite sex. He will be so consumed with the exercise of extortion and power grab that he will never remember he or she is on spiritual assignment. We see such people all over the place, and like Gehazi, they do not always end well.

Submission and loyalty draw from the grace that is upon their leader, and this is one of the ways one catches the spirit of a leader. But once there is a crack in that relationship everything goes south, except something is done almost immediately.

Here was a man who had the potential of connecting with the double portion of grace on Elisha, but he allowed filthy lucre to rob him of kingdom grace. His focus was neither on spiritual elevation by grace, nor enduement of power from on high, all he wanted was material things to consume his lust on. He did not finish well.

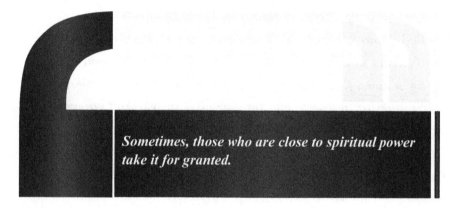

Sometimes, those who are close to spiritual power take it for granted.

Responsibilities
of a Choir

9

CHAPTER

Responsibilities of a Choir

Introduction

The responsibility of a Choir is not to preach or abuse the time allotted to them to minister. As mentioned above, the role of each clan of the Levites does not permit them to jump ship or disrupt the order of service. Simply stay in your lane and be the very best at what is committed into your hands. Remember, the spirit of a prophet is subject to the prophet as seen in 1 Corinthians 14:32 (NIV).

"The spirits of prophets are subject to the control of prophets."

B. The Expectations from the Choir

1. You are expected to Minister:

To serve others first (God, Pastor, Congregation, as they do the work in the Tabernacle). This calls for selflessness at all levels without having chips on your shoulders. Let me use this opportunity to prepare someone who says I have been called into the ministry of worship. You need to be aware of the following salient points.

- Sir or Ma'am, this ministry comes with abuse from all levels and dimensions.

- This ministry will teach you humility but if you remain diligent you will eat the fruit.
- This ministry has a way of teaching one submission and loyalty, if you have teachable spirit, you will see God at work perpetually.

Only remember that your responsibility is to minister first to God, His servant, and His congregation. It is in your doing this that your path to greatness is birthed. Naivety will take you further than you can imagine in this ministry because in Matthew 18:1-5 (NKJV) we are encouraged to be like little children as we serve.

"At that time the disciples came to Jesus, saying, "Who then is greatest in the kingdom of heaven?" Then Jesus called a little child to Him, set him in the midst of them, and said, "Assuredly, I say to you, unless you are converted and become as little children, you will by no means enter the kingdom of heaven. Therefore, whoever humbles himself as this little child is the greatest in the kingdom of heaven. Whoever receives one little child like this in My name receives Me."

Please understand, this ministry does not respect any person, age, or title. You might be the youngest, yet if you engage yourself in the things of the God you have come to minister to, you become the head, and nobody will question it because the evidence is there to prove it. So, in Matthew 23:11-12 (NKJV) we are told:

"But he who is greatest among you shall be your servant. And whoever exalts himself will be humbled, and he who humbles himself will be exalted."

2. You are expected to be Available:

An important responsibility of the Choir is for them to be available for service. Please understand that the availability I am talking about is not just physical, rather it is holistic. Your availability generates power, unity, and so much more.

I am talking about the kind of availability that creates oneness and unity of spirit, birthed in the place of prayer and fellowship, where God is everything and everything is God. Where the team is so spiritually knit that the bond is literally tangible. So, in Joshua 23:10 – 11 (NKJV) the spirit of the Lord spells out what such a bond will bring forth.

"One man of you shall chase a thousand, for the LORD your God is He who fights for you, as He promised you. Therefore take careful heed to yourselves, that you love the LORD your God."

3. You are expected to take Instructions.

If I had my way, I would define the Choir as a place where you are taught to deal with instructions. An unteachable person is unable to because that fellow carries the spirit of rebellion and insubordination and such spirit grieves the Holy Spirit, and much can never be achieved with him or her.

It is the responsibility of the Choir member to always adhere to instructions. Remember, a Choir is a group of people who had chosen to come together as a team to achieve something musically. So, one person cannot go against the agreed instructions that bind them together as they focus on their goal.

That is why in Psalm 50:16-18 (NKJV) we read:

"But to the wicked God says: "What right have you to declare My statutes, Or take My covenant in your mouth, Seeing you hate instruction And cast My words behind you? When you saw a thief, you consented with him, And have been a partaker with adulterers."

If you cannot take instruction what gives you the right to give one? People who would not obey instructions struggle in life. In Proverbs 4:11-13 (NKJV) we read the profound statement:

"I have taught you in the way of wisdom; I have led you in right paths. When you walk, your steps will not be hindered, And when you run, you will not stumble. Take firm hold of instruction, do not let go; Keep her, for she is your life."

4. You are expected to be Accountable:
Another vital responsibility of the Choir is accountability. A church Choir is accountable to God, they are accountable to their Choir leader, and fellow Choir members, both individually and personally.

Accountability is defined as being responsible for accomplishing goals or tasks given. The Choir is no exception as they play a major role in the Church. Since the church and most of her workers are volunteers, this makes it slightly difficult but not impossible to measure or check accountability.

Hence, in Hebrews 4:12-13 (NLT) we are told that: *"For the word of God is alive and powerful. It is sharper than the sharpest two-edged sword, cutting between soul and spirit, between joint and marrow. It exposes our innermost thoughts and desires. Nothing in all creation is hidden from God. Everything is naked and exposed before his eyes, and he is the one to whom we are accountable."*

God becomes the one, who as a member of Choir, we defer our commitment, accountability, or availability to. The case is different if the Choir member is paid by the church. Such a person will not just be held accountable by God but by the reason of employment, such will be made to account for what his or her responsibility is. Generally, every member of the Choir must be accountable to their employer and or spiritual leader as we read in Hebrews 13:17 (NLT):

"Obey your spiritual leaders and do what they say. Their work is to watch over your souls, and they are accountable to God. Give them a reason to do this with joy and not with sorrow. That would certainly not be for your benefit."

5. You are expected to be Committed:
(Be diligent in all your ways).

The shared diligence required in the Choir is out of this world. It takes passion, tenacity, and grace to remain responsible to the call of being in a Choir. This responsibility goes both ways, as it is for the Choir to be committed to their responsibility to the church, the Pastor or the leadership of the church must in turn be responsible to see to the wellbeing of their Choir members or be aware of their present condition, and this should be the case in all other departments of the Church. We are counseled in Proverbs 27:23-24 (NKJV) to:

"Be diligent to know the state of your flocks And attend to your herds; For riches are not forever, Nor does a crown endure to all generations."

6. You are expected to be Sanctified Daily
We know that God desires those who will worship Him in spirit and in truth, so He wants His creation to worship Him.

But the fact remains that there are expectations from God on how He both wants to be worshipped and how He needs to be worshipped. Sanctification is one of the many "How" God wants and needs to be worshipped. Jesus prayed a prayer for all God's children in John 17:16-18 (NKJV):

"They are not of the world, just as I am not of the world. Sanctify them by Your truth. Your word is truth. As You sent Me into the world, I also have sent them into the world."

In the Old Testament, there were rules and regulations guarding lead worship (the Priest), the Choir, and the congregation. The lead worshipper must have separated himself from people for at least seven days seeking consecration before the Lord and praying for sanctification. The same is expected of the singers and worshippers. These are the basic demands and responsibilities of the Choir.

The following Bible references will further show the level of demands placed on the Choir in the Old Testament on the issue of Sanctification. In Leviticus 21:6 to 8 (NLT) we read that:

"They must be set apart as holy to their God and must never bring shame on the name of God. They must be holy, for they are the ones who present special gifts to the Lord, gifts of food for their God. "Priests may not marry a woman defiled by prostitution, and they may not marry a woman who is divorced from her husband, for the priests are set apart as holy to their God. You must treat them as holy because they offer up food to your God. You must consider them holy because I, the Lord, am holy, and I make you holy."

But thank God for Jesus' coming into the picture, now that does not mean that the demand or call for sanctification has been removed, rather Jesus took that constant reminder of man's sin upon Himself and gave grace in return for a worship leader of a Choir to come boldly before God and do that which is always right before God and His people. However, he still needs to watch in prayer to ensure that his garment is not soiled by the sins of the flesh. The Lord Jesus had paid the price, and this is the reason we can approach the throne boldly to obtain mercy and find grace to minister daily (Heb. 4:16). He is our High Priest who offered Himself once and for all for our sins:

"But our High Priest offered himself to God as a single sacrifice for sins, good for all time. Then he sat down in the place of honor at God's right hand." (Heb. 10:12 NLT)

Through His sacrifice for us, we are sanctified and set apart for Him. By entering God's presence on our behalf, He has secured for us an *"eternal redemption"* as Apostle Paul in 1 Timothy 2:5 (NKJV) made us understand:

"For there is one God, and there is one mediator between God and men, the man Christ Jesus."

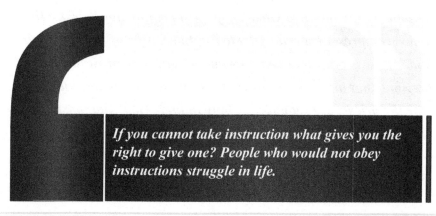

If you cannot take instruction what gives you the right to give one? People who would not obey instructions struggle in life.

Rehearsals Etiquette

CHAPTER **10**

Rehearsals Etiquette

Background

A rehearsal is the pre-worship session practice to make the Choir ready to meet with the King and to bring down His glory as they lead worship. This means rehearsals are equally as important as the worship session itself because the day will reveal the outcome of your rehearsal.

Any act of indiscipline or unpreparedness could ruin the goal of the rehearsal itself. That is the reason why every rehearsal must be taken seriously as it is an assignment with a glorious purpose in mind. Therefore, when you are going for a rehearsal, the following crucial expectations must be adhered to:

1. Be Prayer Filled.
Make it your personal life goal to always pray. Put your house in order and repent of any sin that may hinder the flow of the spirit. Anything that could attract a weak link to the worship must be jettisoned. Therefore, see to it that "...*you offer your bodies as a living sacrifice, holy, and pleasing to God – this is your true and proper worship.*" (Rom 12:1 NIV)

CHAPTER 10

2. Be Punctual.

Always remember that the meeting is an appointment with God and not man. Your behavior before, during, and after Choir meetings is very important. Talking during rehearsals will cause it to go on for too long, as people will repeatedly ask questions that have been addressed earlier. This was because they were not listening or the people chatting did not allow them to hear the information being communicated.

You must learn to score your songs dutifully and privately. Choir rehearsals are not where you come to learn the song, rather, it is where you come to put together the various harmonies of a song. This is because it is expected that you should have done your due diligence by practicing your lines and parts several times and understanding the songs.

You must have practiced either singing the verses or chorus of the song which should make you ready to be in sync with others. This is one way to honor God, value the time of other Choir members, and be an invaluable team player.

3. Pray for your Leader.

Every mistake or error falls back on the leader.

For this reason, sincerely we should uphold him in prayer and not join others to cut him or her down if you notice his or her vulnerability! Yes, leadership is sacrifice, and servanthood takes God's grace to fulfill however, to lead with grace is not impossible. All Choir members must pray for all their leaders because every decision made affects everyone, and through your diligent prayers God's hands may be on your leader to bring forth the mind of God in due season. Moreso, you also must pray for their safety and sanity.

B. The activities of the Choir during Service.

In summary, the activities of the Choir during every service are as follows:

1. They Minister in Songs (secondarily) but Worship God (Primarily)

2. They usher people into God's presence through praise and worship.

3. They are the first point of call or the face of the church.

4. They are expected to always exhibit God's characteristics because they are in His presence and are before the people watching them as well.

5. They must constantly be in-tune with God, or His glory will not descend in that service. Any discordant note or distracted heart is in fellowship with the flesh, and this is unacceptable before the throne of grace.

C. The Backing Vocalist (BV'S)

In the Choir, you have the Worship Lead (the person leading the congregation in worship), then you have a few more people aiding him or her to sing and make the worship more interesting. Those people behind the worship leader are called the Backing Vocalists. The roles of the backing vocalist are itemized below:

1. Backing Vocalist

This *vocalist* provides vocal accompaniment to a lead singer, either live or in a recording studio. He or she oftentimes works with other *backing singers*, singing phrases, providing *harmonies* in a melodic context, or leading into the main vocals. Sometimes a *backing vocalist* may be asked to arrange the *harmonies* of the track.

2. Session Singer

A *session singer* provides both, lead and backing vocals for a specified project based on a *contract*. He or she is invited to take that role because the person is notably skilled at it.

3. Replacement Vocalist

A *replacement vocalist* or *deputizing singer* is someone who acts as a substitute for another singer.

4. Tribute Singer

A *tribute singer* oftentimes impersonates a past or current artist by being able to replicate their singing style and behavior very closely.

5. Lead Vocalist

The *lead vocalist* or *lead singer* is oftentimes the *frontman* (or *frontwoman*) of a *group* or *band* and acts as the most prominent voice in the performance.

6. Solo Artist

A *Solo artist* is basically a *lead vocalist* who performs as an individual, or under his or her individual identity.

D. Qualities of a Good Singer

A singer should be able to do the following:

- Have good pitch and tone when singing a song to an audience.
- Have clear diction in singing and speaking.
- Be able to translate a given song properly.
- Be educated about microphone techniques.
- Have a good understanding of stage etiquette.
- Be able to learn and perform new songs with short rehearsal time.

- Be versatile in his or her ability to perform different music styles.
- Be flexible to make changes to style and performance by instructions.
- Be able to deliver what is expected during a recording session.
- Ability to be consistent in performance when a retake is necessary.
- Have a good listening ear and replicate the melody.
- Have good rhythm control when singing in a group.
- Be able to harmonize or blend with other singers.
- Be able to deliver different harmonies for the purpose of stacking them on top of each other.
- Be able to arrange harmonious parts and backing vocals.

All Choir members must pray for all their leaders because every decision made affects everyone, and through your diligent prayers God's hands may be on your leader to bring forth the mind of God in due season.

The A-Z Tips On Voice Training

CHAPTER
11

Introduction

This chapter is put together as a reference notebook for those interested in the ministry of music or currently learning to grow in it. We can never stop learning. When you stop learning; you start decaying.

This ministry requires intentionality and focus if you must excel in the art of music. Having gone through this path for many years, God has helped me make some notes along the lines that have helped me make a difference.

I am sharing my little insights with you to the glory of God. Join me as we review them together.

A=Articulate.

Using your articulators (lips, teeth, tip of the tongue) more specifically to create your words will help you sing better and more easily. So many of us swallow our articulation (meaning farther back in our mouth) and that habit gets in the way of resonance, tone placement, and other important singing mechanics.

CHAPTER

To improve your skill, quickly say the articulator tongue twister five times in a row: "lips, teeth, the tip of the tongue, lips, teeth, etc." Be sure to really concentrate on exaggerating the movements with the articulators. See where all the action is? That is where you feel the action of articulation when you sing. Keep in mind that you will probably feel like you are moving them in a ridiculous fashion if you are not used to using them actively. Check a mirror, you will probably be surprised.

B = Build Your Song Performance.

Think about how a well-constructed roller coaster builds in intensity and suspense throughout the ride. Your song should have the same sort of ups and downs. For the best results, plan the dynamics (volume and intensity) of your singing. Do not just sing as powerfully as you can from the get-go. Figure out the emotional and natural build of the music and sing accordingly. As an example, using a basic song form, you would do your initial build from Verse 1 through Chorus 1, bring them back a bit for Verse 2 only to get a slightly bigger build (than the peak of Chorus 1) on Chorus 2 before exploding into the bridge. Remember, singing is as much an art form as a skill.

C = Cope with Unexpected Singing Events

And challenges the smart way. Figure out which part of your vocal instrument is out of balance and make an instant adjustment. If you are not sure what makes up your "vocal instrument" you would benefit from learning vocal mechanics.

D = Dare to Try Something Different.

So many singers practice the same song, the same way, over and over and over again. If it did not work the first twenty times, why is it going to work the twenty-first? Try altering different aspects of your singing and attempt to find an easier way to accomplish your best sound. For example, increase/decrease articulation, increase/decrease the amount of airflow, increase/decrease diaphragm support, alter tone placement, alter resonance…get the picture?

E = Energy, not Effort.

This is one of the most confusing concepts in singing. Energy in tone is what we want, and effort is something we want to desperately avoid. Energy is created naturally when our vocal instrument is in balance and our body is involved in the singing process. It feels good. It feels easy. Sometimes it occurs naturally and other times we may have to adjust. The effort usually occurs when singers use their throat muscles/membranes and vocal cords improperly to create volume. We should feel and see very little happening in our throat area if we apply energy in tone.

F = Feathers.

When learning to sing your full range and accomplish the desired one voice (same power with similar tone throughout the whole range) singers often experience cracks and breaks. One way to test this is to practice a siren. Slide on the syllable "he" from the bottom of your range to the top. If you do not experience cracks or breaks, try it on all syllables at all volumes.

When you find yourself faced with this challenge, it is the common response to "try harder" or "give more effort" on those notes. This is not the way to solve this issue. What you want to do is to lighten up just a bit on the notes, and let them float like a feather instead of trying harder and stomping on them.

Understand that most often this is caused because muscles and membranes not having the memory, they need to make the transition you require, as quickly as you want it made. Repetition will give them memory, so keep practicing. Lighten up just a bit on those notes and sing through the break. Do not develop the habit of stopping when you "crack" or it will come back to bite you later.

G = Get Over It and Go for It.

So many talented young singers come into my studio with a good voice and with work, really shine on their vocal skills…but when it comes to performance, they suffer the "**I'm afraid I'll look stupid**" syndrome. Why do we do that? We see music videos and concerts every day when artists give us their all, and yet we feel less stupid singing like a statue than we do really go for it! Makes no sense, but this is not a random occurrence. And unfortunately, when you do not really "perform" the song, you will never be able to give your absolute best performance.

Why? One's performance involves some sort of emotional connection with the song, when you put the emotion on your face and in your body, you will sing completely differently than a statue, no matter how knowledgeable.

H = Humming.

Humming should be easy and sound-alive. If you cannot hum well, you are not singing up to your potential. Humming is a good way to determine which part of your vocal instrument is not warmed up or pulling its weight. When you hum you should be able to feel the resonant vibration on the
front of your face.

I = Increase Your Air Speed

Increase your airspeed for high notes and decrease your airspeed for lower notes. Each frequency requires a specific airspeed to create the absolute best tone. Many singers push too much air, too quickly, while singing low notes to make the note louder. All this does is add stress and tension to the tone. Use your ears to tell you when the proper balance is reached. The tone should sound clear and pure before adding stylistic nuances.

J = Jaw Tension.

Most people do not realize how tense their jaw is because it feels perfectly natural to them. Be sure to stretch out your face and jaw muscles and even make a specific point to monitor your jaw when singing to be sure it truly is relaxed. If your jaw is tense, you will not receive your best tone and perhaps even have trouble hitting some of the higher tones.

K = Keep It Clean.

When practicing your vocal skills focus on creating a pure and clear tone first, free of airiness, rasp, and other tonal changes added for stylistic purposes. If you cannot create a clear tone full of life and energy, you are not singing up to your potential.

L = Lift Your Diaphragm.

So many singers learn to "belly breath" (*breathe into the belly*) and therefore tend to think that lifting their diaphragm feels like holding in their tummy. You can sing like this, but you are only using half your resources and not making full use of the power provided by the muscles in the back. To get your best breath for singing, you want to fill up your abdomen like an inner tube, you should feel expansion all the way around your body...yes, even in your back. Then to compress the air and support the vocal tone release, you lift the diaphragm muscle straight up from the centre of your body. If you are used to the other way, it takes some practice to get the new diaphragm muscle memory, but well worth the effort!

M = Money Notes Matter.

Let's face it. If you are singing a song with a big money note, let's be real. You can knock the rest of the song out of the park, but if you miss the money note that is all your audience will remember. A lot of times singers miss money notes because they are worried about it and if you even think for a moment that it "might not happen" you just increased your odds of it not happening by a great deal.

Usually, it is only one or two notes of a phrase that reach that "money" potential. When you focus specifically on the note, you compartmentalize it and tell your subconscious to watch out for it. Instead, in practice try concentrating on the phrase. Figure out how to use the phrase to your advantage. Sometimes changing your placement on the note(s) just before your money note can make a huge difference. And of course, during performance...see yourself hitting that note like a pro. If you can see it and you believe it, you will hit it almost every time.

N = Never Let Them See You Sweat.

The perception of the audience is the reality. Say that out loud, "the perception of the audience is the reality." What they think is true, is true. So, if you sing with confidence and handle that "creative" phrase you accidentally added like a professional, most of your audience will be convinced that you meant to sing it that way. Professionals sing creative nuances, amateurs make mistakes.

O = One Voice.

If you have been around organized singing groups or perhaps even studied training you have probably heard these terms: chest voice, middle voice, head voice and belt voice. Some singers have even had the misfortune of studying under these kinds of principle unfortunately that usually means they cannot sing very many songs and still sound like one person. When they go up for that higher note in the phrase, they end up switching to some hooty, covered, "head voice" sound. We will not go into the foundation of these terms here but know that your goal as a singer is to manage the balance of resonance in all cavities so you can sing from low to high with a consistent tone.

P = Placement of Your Tone

Refers to where the tone is centred. Mastering tone placement will make your singing incredibly easy and consistent. Some people are born with the skill of good tone placement and others must really work at it. To get technical, there is both a horizontal and vertical placement.

For example: horizontal placement, the tone can be centred at the front of your mouth, the middle, or the back (back never preferred).

For example: vertical placement, draw a line from the middle of your chin to the top middle of your head. The higher the note, the higher the placement.

Q = Quit Singing Through Your Nose.

Nasal tone qualities occur when there is too much resonance in your nasal cavity and not enough sympathetic resonance, or overtones being created in other cavities. One quick fix is to simply open your mouth taller.

R = Resonance.

Resonance is commonly defined as the "*key to your vocal signature.*" As singers, we are far more interested in how we manipulate our singing style or signature. Resonance is created by the sound wave/frequency we create doing singing. It shapes and amplifies the resonating cavity (*chest voice, head voice, nasal voice, throat voice, full belt voice and falsetto voice*). The resonating cavity we have the most control over is the size and shape of our mouth. So, play around with the size and shape of your mouth to hear changes in your resonance. About mouth shape, taller is preferred over wider.

S = Sing the Story.

Singing is acting through song. Why sing the song and not convey the message? Get emotionally involved with the lyrics. Figure out what would make you spontaneously speak the words and sing them with conviction.

T = Think Sing.

The most efficient way to learn a song is to NOT sing it right away. By listening to a song, you can learn what you are supposed to do a lot faster, without creating any bad habits you are only going to have to break later.

If you can think-sing a song from beginning to end, anticipating every breath and melody nuance, then you are ready to sing. It is like a playbook for football. Study the play first before jumping in the game. Not successfully "*think-singing*" the song before you sing it is like a ball player running around the field with no idea of the play.

U = Unify Your Vowels.

You know how you can sing one word on a specific note easily, but another word seems much harder? You could probably use some practice and training on unifying your vowels. The ability to unify your vowels and make them sound as if they come from one instrument, having about the same high and low frequencies, and blended with no cracks or breaks is one skill that separates the accomplished singer from an amateur.

V = Volume and Power.

Volume and power should be gained by using the muscles in the back and abdomen. If you are losing your voice after 4-6 songs or if you hear a lot of "effort" in your tone (it doesn't float in a pure fashion), then you are probably using your throat.

W = Wishing.

Wishing your voice was pro quality will not get it there. You would be surprised what one hour of specific vocal practice five days a week can do. Sorry, this does not usually apply to singing your favourite songs during commute time or singing the same song repeatedly in your bedroom. While you may make some improvement this way, making a productive practice vocal plan would be much more efficient and of course, help you make much faster progress.

X = (E)Exercise Your Voice Regularly.

So many singers shy away from doing voice exercises, claiming they can train and warm up by singing their favorite songs. While some professionals will do this in a pinch, most of them train using exercises and warm up their voices prior to performance the same way. Pros know that warmups will take you through muscle movements that a song never could. Not only will warmups tell you where your voice is, as in "not awake", but using them during training can help you develop necessary muscle memory for difficult passages you encounter later.

Here is another quick tip…when you go to sing your song, you should be singing it the same way you sing during the vocal exercises. Most of us will exercise with good placement, support, resonance, etc., but when we add words and our favorite melody all that goes out the window. Work at being consistent. If we were football quarterbacks, would we practice throwing the ball one way and then throw it completely differently during a real game? I don't think so.

Y = Your Style.

So many students avoid improving certain mechanical skills because they claim that it is their style. While it is true that certain things singers do, the shape of their mouth, how they pronounce words, etc., contributes to their signature voice. Improving how you create your tone will only make your signature voice better. Do not back away from understanding your voice; learn all you can about your instrument to create your best sound.

Z = Zen.

Sometimes we cannot help but let our emotions and personal life circumstances affect our performances. We are human, after all. However, with practice and meditation, you can learn to clear your head and totally focus on connecting with your song and the appropriate emotions of your selection, instead of whatever else was distracting you. Your body language and expression communicate your focus…but it is your eyes that communicate your thoughts most of all.

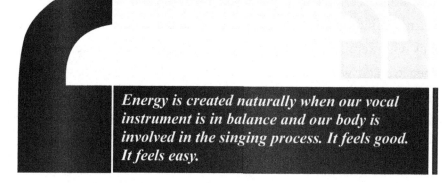

Energy is created naturally when our vocal instrument is in balance and our body is involved in the singing process. It feels good. It feels easy.

Making The Right Choices

CHAPTER 12

As I begin to draw a conclusion to this book titled "**The dynamics of a worship Leader**" it dawned on me that this book is about a person and his God. It is about a person who has chosen to deliberately serve or please his or her master, in this case, God Almighty.

This book is about the choices and methodologies one has decided to use to do better in life as one pursues God in holiness and practicalizes it in their daily living. A choice not forced but chosen so that life can be meaningful in every ramification.

Worship is what you make of it, be it a myth or a misconstrued thought, it is what you make of it that gives it meaning. But that does not change the following facts:

1. Worship is real.
2. God wants to be worshipped.
3. If one is not worshipping God, one is worshipping something other than God. There can never be a grey area.
4. It is our choice to make if we worship God or not. But like Moses, I encourage you to worship Him, for that is life itself.

The Lord is not expecting you and me to be perfect when we come to the realization of who we are and how we have been, but He expects us to put in effort in all our endeavors in pursuit of Him. In the New Testament alone, we were told to *"make every effort"* in our growth toward becoming like Jesus Christ seven times. Why? Because Jesus Christ became the standard, the yardstick that all men must emulate in desiring to worship God.

Below are the seven scriptures that encourage us to make effort to be like Jesus Christ, and each of these scriptures brought a measure of what God requires of a worshipper after His heart like David.

1. In Luke 13:24 (NLT); we were informed that it will take *"Hard Work"* to get the desired intimacy with God as it reads: *"Work hard to enter the narrow door to God's Kingdom, for many will try to enter but will fail."*

2. In Romans 14:19 (NLT), we are told that to be a dynamic worshipper, it will take *"Harmony and Oneness"* to get it right. This is because God is in the business of building and uniting people for His glory. The scripture reads: *"So then, let us aim for harmony in the church and try to build each other up."*

3. Ephesians 4:3 (NLT) informs us that the *"Unity in Spirit"* both with God and man brings peace. The verse says, *"Make every effort to keep yourselves united in the Spirit, binding yourselves together with peace."*

1. "*Enter that Rest*" only found in worshipping God. So, the scripture reads; "*So let us do our best to enter that rest. But if we disobey God, as the people of Israel did, we will fall.*"

2. In Hebrews 12:14 (NLT), we were encouraged to live both a "*Peaceable and a Holy Life*", as they are required if we truly want to be dynamic worship leader. The scripture reads; "*Work at living in peace with everyone, and work at living a holy life, for those who are not holy will not see the Lord.*"

3. In 2 Peter 3:14 (NLT) we are enjoined to live a "*Pure and Blameless life*" as this is a requirement to be a dynamic worship leader. The verse reads: "*And so, dear friends, while you are waiting for these things to happen, make every effort to be found living peaceful lives that are pure and blameless in his sight.*"

Stemming from all that we have read and seen; becoming a dynamic worship leader is not what one sits around and waits to assume will happen magically. Apostle Paul explains in Ephesians 4:22 to 24, that we have three responsibilities in becoming a dynamic worship leader as showcased by our Lord Jesus Christ. It reads:

"*throw off your old sinful nature and your former way of life, which is corrupted by lust and deception. Instead, let the Spirit renew your thoughts and attitudes. Put on your new nature, created to be like God - truly righteous and holy.*"

The above scripture highlighted three points and it is wise to break these points down for better understanding.

Firstly, it encourages us to let go of our pasts, the old ways of acting, and living, and the negative choices we made. The Message translation of Ephesians 4:22 puts it like this,

"Everything - and I do mean everything - connected with that old way of life has to go. It's rotten through and through. Get rid of it!"

Secondly, it addresses our mindset. How we think matters, as it must be changed if we really want to be the person God needs us to be. Verse 23 of Ephesians 4 (CEV), says,

"Let the Spirit change your way of thinking".

Romans 12:2 (NKJV), reads; we are *"transformed" by the renewing of our minds…"*

The word *"transformed"* is a Greek word from the word **"metamorphosis"**. It is used today to describe the amazing change a caterpillar goes through in becoming a butterfly. It is a beautiful picture of what happens to us spiritually when we allow God to direct our thoughts: We are changed from the inside out, and we become more beautiful.

Thirdly, our character must change, by developing new godly habits. One's character is essentially the sum of one's habits. One's habit is how life is to that person. The Bible in Ephesians 4:24 (NIV) says,

"Put on the new self, created to be like God in true righteousness and holiness."

To become a Dynamic Worship Leader, total obedience is required at all levels, this is so that one can unlock God's power and connectivity to Him in our life!

Obedience is uncomfortable, but it is a good and godly thing to do.

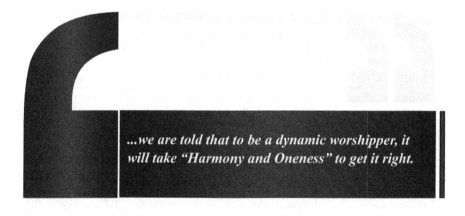

...we are told that to be a dynamic worshipper, it will take "Harmony and Oneness" to get it right.

Biblography

■   All Scripture quotations are taken from Biblegateway.com. Translations: The King James Version (KJV), The New King James Version (NKJV), English Standard Version (ESV), New International Version (NIV), or The New Living Translation Bible (NLT).

■   Web Dictionary

Copyright © 2022 by Gabriel Eziashi

Merriam-Webster Dictionary

Daily Devotional titled: Transformation

By Rick Warren

For more information please visit:

YouTube *YouTube.com/gabrieleziash1*

🌐 *gabrieleziashi.com*

📷 *instagram.com/gabrieleziashi*

f *Facebook.com/gabrieleziashi*

Made in the USA
Middletown, DE
27 October 2023

41475675R10073